Beginning Elastic Stack

Vishal Sharma

Apress®

Beginning Elastic Stack

Vishal Sharma
New Delhi, Delhi
India

ISBN-13 (pbk): 978-1-4842-1693-4   ISBN-13 (electronic): 978-1-4842-1694-1
DOI 10.1007/978-1-4842-1694-1

Library of Congress Control Number: 2016961231

Managing Director: Welmoed Spahr
Acquisitions Editor: Louise Corrigan
Technical Reviewer: Panayiotis Gotsis
Editorial Board: Steve Anglin, Pramila Balan, Laura Berendson, Aaron Black, Louise Corrigan,
    Jonathan Gennick, Todd Green, Robert Hutchinson, Celestin Suresh John, Nikhil Karkal,
    James Markham, Susan McDermott, Matthew Moodie, Natalie Pao, Gwenan Spearing
Coordinating Editor: Nancy Chen
Copy Editor: Michael G. Laraque
Compositor: SPi Global
Indexer: SPi Global
Artist: SPi Global

Distributed to the book trade worldwide by Springer Science+Business Media New York, 233 Spring Street, 6th Floor, New York, NY 10013. Phone 1-800-SPRINGER, fax (201) 348-4505, e-mail orders-ny@springer-sbm.com, or visit www.springer.com. Apress Media, LLC is a California LLC and the sole member (owner) is Springer Science + Business Media Finance Inc (SSBM Finance Inc). SSBM Finance Inc is a **Delaware** corporation.

For information on translations, please e-mail rights@apress.com, or visit www.apress.com.

Apress and friends of ED books may be purchased in bulk for academic, corporate, or promotional use. eBook versions and licenses are also available for most titles. For more information, reference our Special Bulk Sales–eBook Licensing web page at www.apress.com/bulk-sales.

Any source code or other supplementary materials referenced by the author in this text are available to readers at www.apress.com. For detailed information about how to locate your book's source code, go to www.apress.com/source-code/. Readers can also access source code at SpringerLink in the Supplementary Material section for each chapter.

Printed on acid-free paper

Contents at a Glance

Contents

About the Author

Vishal Sharma is a developer and entrepreneur with more than ten years' experience working with various GNU/Linux server distributions and open source tools. As well as Logstash, he enjoys exploring server and web application security, to stay ahead of hackers and spammers and protect clients' data.

About the Technical Reviewer

Panayiotis Gotysis has been working with systems and system administration since the moment he understood the power and magic of the CLI. For the past 12 years, he has specialized in architecting systems for redundancy, high availability and security, with an emphasis on virtualization and storage technologies.

In the last 3 years, working for the Greek Research Network (https://www.grnet.gr), he has moved into the DevOps mindset, seeking for configuration management, automation, and orchestration. Puppet and the ELK stack form the staple of the Greek Research Network's operations as their service portfolio expands and their cloud offering, based on Ganeti (http://www.ganeti.org/) and Synnefo (https://www.synnefo.org/) provides virtualized resources to the academic and research institutions in Greece.

His current interests lie in architecting disaster recovery solutions, working with Fabric (http://www.fabfile.org/) and using these tools to perform capacity management.

When not on a keyboard, he likes to improve his amateur photography skills and roll d20s with his role playing group.

Panayiotis can be reached at panos@gotsis.info.

Acknowledgments

I would like to thank a few special people:

- I would first like to thank my Mom, Mrs. Rama Pachauri, without her continuous support and love I never would have been able to finish the book.

- A special thanks to my Dad, Mr. V.C Pachauri for letting me do whatever I want to, and for providing me the much needed support always.

- I can't thank enough to my wife Shweta for giving me the much needed confidence and the courage to complete the book. There was a rough time when I was caught between my business and completing the book and Shweta was always there with suggestions and support.

- I'd like to thank my friends Gaurav Mahajan, Hemant Gaba & Yakesh Arora for being pillars of my life over the years.

- A big thank you to Panos for helping me out with the Technical Review and suggestions which helped me to include more technical things.

- I want to thank Thomas d'Otreppe (Author Aircrack-ng) for doing Technical Review of my book. Man you are my hero, thank you so much for your help.

- Thanks to Louise from Apress for giving me an opportunity and for helping me out with everything.

- Nancy from Apress thanks for the push I needed.

Introduction

Back in 2005 when I have started my career as a server administrator in a startup, I had just 2 servers to manage. That was an easy job with just few websites running on both the servers. However, in next few years I had more than 10 servers running with different application and services. So I had to check the logs of every server and it was like spending more than a half day every day. Slowly the number of servers increased so I have configured few scripts to send me some important log information of each server, but again in just next 1 year I had 50+ servers to manage and it was crazy checking logs and I was worried, as there were all kinds of attacks happening on the servers. It was a huge task to read logs and troubleshooting the issues for each server, all I wanted was to have a centralized log server. I googled and found Logstash, as I was learning more about Logstash I came across with Elasticsearch & Kibana as well and it was a wow moment for me.

I have configured the ELK setup and started working on it. The whole experience was amazing, I was able to configure all the service logs and application log to a centralized server and also was able to define the parameters I wanted. The setup helped me to quickly search through the logs and find out the issues. Using the plugins, I have configured alerts as well.

There is a good community support and the product is keep evolving even to this date. The book Beginning Elastic Stack covers everything to configure a centralized log server quickly and effectively. In the book I have also covered Elastic Stack setup with Puppet and Foreman, which will help the server administrators not to just having ELK Stack configured quickly and easily but also having a system managing servers using Puppet.

CHAPTER 1

■ ■ ■

Getting Started with Logstash

Logstash is an open source tool designed to manage all of your server logs in a centralized location. This book includes detailed examples and insights that will help the novice install Logstash and use it like a pro. The book will also cover the other components of ELK Stack, such as Elasticsearch, Kibana, and Watcher and Shield. For this book, CentOS 7 and Ubuntu 16.0.4.1 LTS test server machines are Linode servers available from www.linode.com.

Why Use Logstash?

Log management is often a tedious task for server administrators. It's a nightmare if you are managing multiple servers with many services and web apps running that are crucial for your business. The situation is even worse if you have hundreds of hosts and multiple log files with which you must work.

Imagine a situation in which on a Monday morning, you have reached your office and your boss immediately calls you in and says that there has been a major problem with your company's web sites over the weekend. They are running very slow, or perhaps some of them went offline completely. Of course, you are upset, and you return to your workstation and start the long process of checking the logs, starting with GNU/Linux commands, such as grep or tail, or writing shell scripts to extract the information from the logs.

You begin by looking at secure logs, Apache logs, database logs, firewall logs, and so on, to locate the problem and investigate it. You might eventually find something, but the amount of time and effort this requires is just too much. Also, you may not have all of the necessary information.

There are tools available, such as syslog-ng, which are helpful but, again, require that you spend hours of your time finding everything, as the logs grow larger.

You need something that can parse your logs properly and efficiently. You need a tool with which you can search the strings and quickly find the results. Moreover, you need a tool that acts as a centralized logging system for your servers. Fortunately, Logstash is an excellent tool for doing just this.

Logstash is an open source tool developed by Jordan Sissel, who currently works for Elastic. Logstash acts as a data pipeline through which it processes the data from multiple servers and systems. Logstash can take inputs from TCP/UDP protocols, files, and log management systems, such as syslog-ng, rsyslog, and many more tools in the field that server administrators install to analyze server events. Like Puppet and CFEngine, or with monitoring systems like Nagios, Graphite & Zabbix.

For example, let's say that you have a few servers running at different locations, and these are clusters or load-balancing servers for your web app. The beauty of Logstash is that it can be used in this scenario, as it allows you to have a master server wherein all of these nodes can send log data, and you can see and search the logs from this master machine. Isn't that an amazing setup? Indeed, it is!

Electronic supplementary material The online version of this chapter (doi:10.1007/978-1-4842-1694-1_1) contains supplementary material, which is available to authorized users.

Logstash, Elasticsearch, and Kibana Setup

The servers that are running Logstash agents are called *shippers*. They send log events of your applications and services to the Logstash server.

The central Logstash server running services such as brokers, indexers, and storage interface with Kibana, which is a visualization tool.

Figure 1-1 illustrates how the Logstash, Elasticsearch, and Kibana setup works. We will explore the entire setup in greater depth in later chapters.

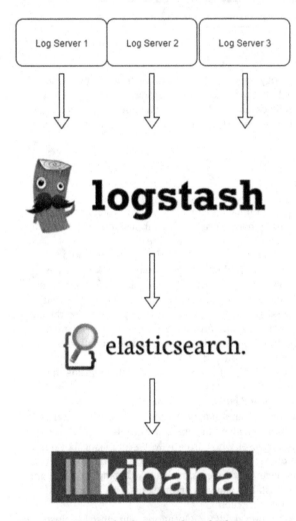

Figure 1-1. *Logstash, Elasticsearch, and Kibana setup*

Logstash collects data from the different sources defined by using the configuration file. Logstash can process any type of logs that are being maintained, including Apache logs, MySQL logs, firewall logs, and error logs. The best part is that one can store logs from different nodes and services in a centralized place and analyze them there.

Elasticsearch does real-time data analysis from different data sources. It is scalable, and it does full text search.

Kibana is a web application designed to visualize data in Elasticsearch. It allows you to search data (in our case, logs) and visualize it in various ways (such as bar graph, pie charts, and other graph types). Visualizations can be organized in dashboards for quick access to information.

Following are some of Logstash's key features:

- Logstash is open source and free to use.

- Logstash is lightweight.

- Logstash is highly customizable.

- Logstash is easy to configure.

- Input and output plug-ins are readily available for Logstash.

Preinstallation Setup

Now let's start the process of installing Logstash. I will be covering the Linux distributions CentOS 7 and Ubuntu 16.04.1. Before you start installing Logstash on your machines, you have to install Java, as Logstash is written in JRuby, and you must have a Java Development Kit (JDK) installed. You can install OpenJDK 7 or later versions and can also use the official Oracle version. Here, I prefer working with OpenJDK, as you can install it easily using yum on CentOS and APT on Ubuntu.

Hardware Requirements

You might be setting up the ELK Stack for a production environment in which you are processing much data from different sources. Also, in later chapters, we will be installing more packages and processing more data. Following, therefore, are the minimum hardware requirements:

- 4GB RAM (8GB recommended)

- SSD hard drive (storage amount can be anything depending on your usage)

- Multiple core CPU

- Fast and reliable network. Most data centers have good network speed these days.

Install a Fresh Server

Install a fresh server using CentOS or Ubuntu. Before we proceed with installing the packages, I assume that the user is installing the packages as user and not as root. It is always a good idea to use a GNU/Linux server as user and not as root.

To install the packages as user, you have to use a sudo command. The following link shows you how to configure sudo and how to add user into a sudoers file:

For CentOS

https://wiki.centos.org/TipsAndTricks/BecomingRoot

For Ubuntu

https://help.ubuntu.com/community/RootSudo

Installing OpenJDK 8 and JRE on CentOS 7

If you are installing OpenJDK 8 and JRE, do so as user. On a CentOS or Ubuntu machine, open the terminal from your KDE or Gnome window manager. You will see a screen similar to the one shown in Figure 1-2.

Figure 1-2. *Connect remote server using SSH*

If you are working remotely, SSH into the remote system, which is illustrated in Figure 1-3. Always check for updates on a freshly installed server, as follows:

```
[vishne0@localhost ~]$ sudo yum check-update
[vishne0@localhost ~]$ sudo yum update
```

```
[vishne0@localhost ~]$ sudo yum install java-1.8.0-openjdk
Loaded plugins: fastestmirror
Loading mirror speeds from cached hostfile
 * base: mirrors.linode.com
 * extras: mirrors.linode.com
 * updates: mirrors.linode.com
Resolving Dependencies
--> Running transaction check
---> Package java-1.8.0-openjdk.x86_64 1:1.8.0.102-1.b14.el7_2 will be installed
--> Processing Dependency: java-1.8.0-openjdk-headless = 1:1.8.0.102-1.b14.el7_2 for package: 1:java-1.8.0-openjdk-1.8.0.102-1.b14.el7_2.x86_64
--> Processing Dependency: xorg-x11-fonts-Type1 for package: 1:java-1.8.0-openjdk-1.8.0.102-1.b14.el7_2.x86_64
--> Processing Dependency: libpng15.so.15(PNG15_0)(64bit) for package: 1:java-1.8.0-openjdk-1.8.0.102-1.b14.el7_2.x86_64
--> Processing Dependency: libjvm.so(SUNWprivate_1.1)(64bit) for package: 1:java-1.8.0-openjdk-1.8.0.102-1.b14.el7_2.x86_64
--> Processing Dependency: libjpeg.so.62(LIBJPEG_6.2)(64bit) for package: 1:java-1.8.0-openjdk-1.8.0.102-1.b14.el7_2.x86_64
--> Processing Dependency: libjli.so(SUNWprivate_1.1)(64bit) for package: 1:java-1.8.0-openjdk-1.8.0.102-1.b14.el7_2.x86_64
--> Processing Dependency: libjava.so(SUNWprivate_1.1)(64bit) for package: 1:java-1.8.0-openjdk-1.8.0.102-1.b14.el7_2.x86_64
--> Processing Dependency: libasound.so.2(ALSA_0.9.0rc4)(64bit) for package: 1:java-1.8.0-openjdk-1.8.0.102-1.b14.el7_2.x86_64
--> Processing Dependency: libasound.so.2(ALSA_0.9)(64bit) for package: 1:java-1.8.0-openjdk-1.8.0.102-1.b14.el7_2.x86_64
--> Processing Dependency: fontconfig for package: 1:java-1.8.0-openjdk-1.8.0.102-1.b14.el7_2.x86_64
--> Processing Dependency: libpng15.so.15()(64bit) for package: 1:java-1.8.0-openjdk-1.8.0.102-1.b14.el7_2.x86_64
--> Processing Dependency: libjvm.so()(64bit) for package: 1:java-1.8.0-openjdk-1.8.0.102-1.b14.el7_2.x86_64
--> Processing Dependency: libjpeg.so.62()(64bit) for package: 1:java-1.8.0-openjdk-1.8.0.102-1.b14.el7_2.x86_64
--> Processing Dependency: libjli.so()(64bit) for package: 1:java-1.8.0-openjdk-1.8.0.102-1.b14.el7_2.x86_64
--> Processing Dependency: libjava.so()(64bit) for package: 1:java-1.8.0-openjdk-1.8.0.102-1.b14.el7_2.x86_64
--> Processing Dependency: libgif.so.4()(64bit) for package: 1:java-1.8.0-openjdk-1.8.0.102-1.b14.el7_2.x86_64
--> Processing Dependency: libawt.so()(64bit) for package: 1:java-1.8.0-openjdk-1.8.0.102-1.b14.el7_2.x86_64
--> Processing Dependency: libasound.so.2()(64bit) for package: 1:java-1.8.0-openjdk-1.8.0.102-1.b14.el7_2.x86_64
--> Processing Dependency: libXtst.so.6()(64bit) for package: 1:java-1.8.0-openjdk-1.8.0.102-1.b14.el7_2.x86_64
--> Processing Dependency: libXrender.so.1()(64bit) for package: 1:java-1.8.0-openjdk-1.8.0.102-1.b14.el7_2.x86_64
--> Processing Dependency: libXi.so.6()(64bit) for package: 1:java-1.8.0-openjdk-1.8.0.102-1.b14.el7_2.x86_64
--> Processing Dependency: libXext.so.6()(64bit) for package: 1:java-1.8.0-openjdk-1.8.0.102-1.b14.el7_2.x86_64
--> Processing Dependency: libX11.so.6()(64bit) for package: 1:java-1.8.0-openjdk-1.8.0.102-1.b14.el7_2.x86_64
--> Running transaction check
---> Package alsa-lib.x86_64 0:1.0.28-2.el7 will be installed
---> Package fontconfig.x86_64 0:2.10.95-7.el7 will be installed
--> Processing Dependency: freetype for package: fontconfig-2.10.95-7.el7.x86_64
--> Processing Dependency: fontpackages-filesystem for package: fontconfig-2.10.95-7.el7.x86_64
--> Processing Dependency: libfreetype.so.6()(64bit) for package: fontconfig-2.10.95-7.el7.x86_64
---> Package giflib.x86_64 0:4.1.6-9.el7 will be installed
--> Processing Dependency: libSM.so.6()(64bit) for package: giflib-4.1.6-9.el7.x86_64
--> Processing Dependency: libICE.so.6()(64bit) for package: giflib-4.1.6-9.el7.x86_64
---> Package java-1.8.0-openjdk-headless.x86_64 1:1.8.0.102-1.b14.el7_2 will be installed
--> Processing Dependency: tzdata-java >= 2015d for package: 1:java-1.8.0-openjdk-headless-1.8.0.102-1.b14.el7_2.x86_64
--> Processing Dependency: lksctp-tools for package: 1:java-1.8.0-openjdk-headless-1.8.0.102-1.b14.el7_2.x86_64
```

Figure 1-3. *Installing Java*

Use the following commands in the terminal to install the packages.

```
[vishne0@localhost ~]$ sudo yum install java-1.8.0-openjdk
```

Press Enter, and then type Y to install all the dependencies, along with the OpenJDK JRE to be installed. To install OpenJDK 8 JDK, run the following command:

```
[vishne0@localhost ~]$ sudo yum install java-1.8.0-openjdk-devel
```

Press Enter, and sudo will ask for your password before proceeding further. Enter your password, then type Y. It will now install OpenJDK, as shown in Figure 1-4.

```
[vishne0@localhost ~]$ sudo yum install java-1.8.0-openjdk-devel
Loaded plugins: fastestmirror
Loading mirror speeds from cached hostfile
 * base: mirrors.linode.com
 * extras: mirrors.linode.com
 * updates: mirrors.linode.com
Resolving Dependencies
--> Running transaction check
---> Package java-1.8.0-openjdk-devel.x86_64 1:1.8.0.102-1.b14.el7_2 will be installed
--> Finished Dependency Resolution

Dependencies Resolved

================================================================================
 Package                    Arch        Version                  Repository   Size
================================================================================
Installing:
 java-1.8.0-openjdk-devel   x86_64      1:1.8.0.102-1.b14.el7_2  updates     9.8 M

Transaction Summary
================================================================================
Install  1 Package

Total download size: 9.8 M
Installed size: 40 M
Is this ok [y/d/N]: y
Downloading packages:
java-1.8.0-openjdk-devel-1.8.0.102-1.b14.el7_2.x86_64.rpm        | 9.8 MB  00:00:00
Running transaction check
Running transaction test
Transaction test succeeded
Running transaction
  Installing : 1:java-1.8.0-openjdk-devel-1.8.0.102-1.b14.el7_2.x86_64        1/1
  Verifying  : 1:java-1.8.0-openjdk-devel-1.8.0.102-1.b14.el7_2.x86_64        1/1

Installed:
  java-1.8.0-openjdk-devel.x86_64 1:1.8.0.102-1.b14.el7_2

Complete!
[vishne0@localhost ~]$
```

Figure 1-4. *Installing OpenJDK 8 and JRE on CentOS 7*

Installing OpenJDK 8 and JRE on Ubuntu 16.04.1 LTS

Always upgrade a freshly installed server. To upgrade Ubuntu 16.04.1 LTS, we will run following commands:

```
vishne0@snf-725572:~$ sudo apt-get update
vishne0@snf-725572:~$ sudo apt-get upgrade
```

On some servers, OpenJDK 8 comes preinstalled in Ubuntu 16.04.1 LTS, but you should still check it out to be sure. Open your terminal and issue the following commands:

```
vishne0@snf-725572:~$ java -version
openjdk version "xxxx"
OpenJDK Runtime Environment (build 1.8.0_111-8u111-b14-2ubuntu0.16.04.2-b14)
OpenJDK 64-Bit Server VM (build 25.111-b14, mixed mode)
```

For me, it's already installed. However, if you do not see the preceding output, follow these instructions:

```
vishneo@:~$ sudo apt-get install openjdk-8-jre
```

This command will show you all the dependencies that have to be installed with the package, as shown in Figure 1-5.

```
vishne0@snf-725572:~$ sudo apt-get install openjdk-8-jre
Reading package lists... Done
Building dependency tree
Reading state information... Done
The following additional packages will be installed:
  ca-certificates-java dbus-x11 fontconfig fontconfig-config fonts-dejavu-core fonts-dejavu-extra gconf-service gconf-service-backend gconf2 gconf2-common
  hicolor-icon-theme java-common libasound2 libasound2-data libasyncns0 libatk1.0-0 libatk1.0-data libavahi-client3 libavahi-common-data libavahi-common3
  libavahi-glib1 libbonobo2-0 libbonobo2-common libcairo2 libcanberra0 libcups2 libdatrie1 libdrm-amdgpu1 libdrm-intel1 libdrm-nouveau2 libdrm-radeon1 libflac8
  libfontconfig1 libgconf-2-4 libgdk-pixbuf2.0-0 libgdk-pixbuf2.0-common libgif7 libgl1-mesa-dri libgl1-mesa-glx libglapi-mesa libgnome-2-0 libgnome2-common
  libgnomevfs2-0 libgnomevfs2-common libgraphite2-3 libgtk2.0-0 libgtk2.0-bin libgtk2.0-common libharfbuzz0b libjbig0 libjpeg-turbo8 libjpeg8 liblcms2-2 libllvm3.8
  libltdl7 libnspr4 libnss3 libnss3-nssdb libogg0 liborbit-2-0 libpango-1.0-0 libpangocairo-1.0-0 libpangoft2-1.0-0 libpciaccess0 libpixman-1-0 libpulse0 libsndfile1
  libtdb1 libthai-data libthai0 libtiff5 libxc-dxtn-s2tc0 libvorbis0a libvorbisenc2 libvorbisfile3 libx11-xcb1 libxcb-dri2-0 libxcb-dri3-0 libxcb-glx0
  libxcb-present0 libxcb-render0 libxcb-shm0 libxcb-sync1 libxcomposite1 libxcursor1 libxdamage1 libxfixes3 libxi6 libxinerama1 libxrandr2 libxrender1 libxshmfence1
  libxtst6 libxxf86vm1 openjdk-8-jre-headless sound-theme-freedesktop x11-common
Suggested packages:
  gconf-defaults-service default-jre libasound2-plugins alsa-utils libbonobo2-bin libcanberra-gtk0 libcanberra-pulse cups-common desktop-base libgnomevfs2-bin
  libgnomevfs2-extra gamin | fam gnome-mime-data librsvg2-common gvfs liblcms2-utils pulseaudio icedtea-8-plugin openjdk-8-jre-jamvm libnss-mdns fonts-ipafont-gothic
  fonts-ipafont-mincho ttf-wqy-microhei | ttf-wqy-zenhei fonts-indic
The following NEW packages will be installed:
  ca-certificates-java dbus-x11 fontconfig fontconfig-config fonts-dejavu-core fonts-dejavu-extra gconf-service gconf-service-backend gconf2 gconf2-common
  hicolor-icon-theme java-common libasound2 libasound2-data libasyncns0 libatk1.0-0 libatk1.0-data libavahi-client3 libavahi-common-data libavahi-common3
  libavahi-glib1 libbonobo2-0 libbonobo2-common libcairo2 libcanberra0 libcups2 libdatrie1 libdrm-amdgpu1 libdrm-intel1 libdrm-nouveau2 libdrm-radeon1 libflac8
  libfontconfig1 libgconf-2-4 libgdk-pixbuf2.0-0 libgdk-pixbuf2.0-common libgif7 libgl1-mesa-dri libgl1-mesa-glx libglapi-mesa libgnome-2-0 libgnome2-common
  libgnomevfs2-0 libgnomevfs2-common libgraphite2-3 libgtk2.0-0 libgtk2.0-bin libgtk2.0-common libharfbuzz0b libjbig0 libjpeg-turbo8 libjpeg8 liblcms2-2 libllvm3.8
  libltdl7 libnspr4 libnss3 libnss3-nssdb libogg0 liborbit-2-0 libpango-1.0-0 libpangocairo-1.0-0 libpangoft2-1.0-0 libpciaccess0 libpixman-1-0 libpulse0 libsndfile1
  libtdb1 libthai-data libthai0 libtiff5 libxc-dxtn-s2tc0 libvorbis0a libvorbisenc2 libvorbisfile3 libx11-xcb1 libxcb-dri2-0 libxcb-dri3-0 libxcb-glx0
  libxcb-present0 libxcb-render0 libxcb-shm0 libxcb-sync1 libxcomposite1 libxcursor1 libxdamage1 libxfixes3 libxi6 libxinerama1 libxrandr2 libxrender1 libxshmfence1
  libxtst6 libxxf86vm1 openjdk-8-jre openjdk-8-jre-headless sound-theme-freedesktop x11-common
0 upgraded, 98 newly installed, 0 to remove and 3 not upgraded.
Need to get 53.8 MB of archives.
After this operation, 299 MB of additional disk space will be used.
Do you want to continue? [Y/n] y
Get:1 http://ftp.cc.uoc.gr/mirrors/linux/ubuntu/packages xenial/main amd64 fonts-dejavu-core all 2.35-1 [1,039 kB]
Get:2 http://ftp.cc.uoc.gr/mirrors/linux/ubuntu/packages xenial-updates/main amd64 fontconfig-config all 2.11.94-0ubuntu1.1 [49.9 kB]
Get:3 http://ftp.cc.uoc.gr/mirrors/linux/ubuntu/packages xenial-updates/main amd64 libfontconfig1 amd64 2.11.94-0ubuntu1.1 [131 kB]
Get:4 http://ftp.cc.uoc.gr/mirrors/linux/ubuntu/packages xenial-updates/main amd64 fontconfig amd64 2.11.94-0ubuntu1.1 [178 kB]
Get:5 http://ftp.cc.uoc.gr/mirrors/linux/ubuntu/packages xenial/main amd64 libasyncns0 amd64 0.8-5build1 [12.3 kB]
Get:6 http://ftp.cc.uoc.gr/mirrors/linux/ubuntu/packages xenial/main amd64 libbonobo2-common all 2.32.1-3 [34.7 kB]
Get:7 http://ftp.cc.uoc.gr/mirrors/linux/ubuntu/packages xenial/main amd64 liborbit-2-0 amd64 1:2.14.19-1build1 [140 kB]
Get:8 http://ftp.cc.uoc.gr/mirrors/linux/ubuntu/packages xenial/main amd64 libbonobo2-0 amd64 2.32.1-3 [211 kB]
Get:9 http://ftp.cc.uoc.gr/mirrors/linux/ubuntu/packages xenial/main amd64 libjpeg-turbo8 amd64 1.4.2-0ubuntu3 [111 kB]
Get:10 http://ftp.cc.uoc.gr/mirrors/linux/ubuntu/packages xenial/main amd64 liblcms2-2 amd64 2.6-3ubuntu2 [137 kB]
Get:11 http://ftp.cc.uoc.gr/mirrors/linux/ubuntu/packages xenial/main amd64 libogg0 amd64 1.3.2-1 [17.2 kB]
Get:12 http://ftp.cc.uoc.gr/mirrors/linux/ubuntu/packages xenial/main amd64 libxcomposite1 amd64 1:0.4.4-1 [7,714 B]
```

Figure 1-5. *All the package OpenJDK dependencies*

Press Enter and then press Y (see Figure 1-6).

```
Do you want to continue? [Y/n] y
Get:1 http://ftp.cc.uoc.gr/mirrors/linux/ubuntu/packages xenial/main amd64 fonts-dejavu-core all 2.35-1 [1,039 kB]
Get:2 http://ftp.cc.uoc.gr/mirrors/linux/ubuntu/packages xenial-updates/main amd64 fontconfig-config all 2.11.94-0ubuntu1.1 [49.9 kB]
Get:3 http://ftp.cc.uoc.gr/mirrors/linux/ubuntu/packages xenial-updates/main amd64 libfontconfig1 amd64 2.11.94-0ubuntu1.1 [131 kB]
Get:4 http://ftp.cc.uoc.gr/mirrors/linux/ubuntu/packages xenial-updates/main amd64 fontconfig amd64 2.11.94-0ubuntu1.1 [178 kB]
Get:5 http://ftp.cc.uoc.gr/mirrors/linux/ubuntu/packages xenial/main amd64 libasyncns0 amd64 0.8-5build1 [12.3 kB]
Get:6 http://ftp.cc.uoc.gr/mirrors/linux/ubuntu/packages xenial/main amd64 libbonobo2-common all 2.32.1-3 [34.7 kB]
Get:7 http://ftp.cc.uoc.gr/mirrors/linux/ubuntu/packages xenial/main amd64 liborbit-2-0 amd64 1:2.14.19-1build1 [140 kB]
Get:8 http://ftp.cc.uoc.gr/mirrors/linux/ubuntu/packages xenial/main amd64 libbonobo2-0 amd64 2.32.1-3 [211 kB]
Get:9 http://ftp.cc.uoc.gr/mirrors/linux/ubuntu/packages xenial/main amd64 libjpeg-turbo8 amd64 1.4.2-0ubuntu3 [111 kB]
Get:10 http://ftp.cc.uoc.gr/mirrors/linux/ubuntu/packages xenial/main amd64 liblcms2-2 amd64 2.6-3ubuntu2 [137 kB]
Get:11 http://ftp.cc.uoc.gr/mirrors/linux/ubuntu/packages xenial/main amd64 libogg0 amd64 1.3.2-1 [17.2 kB]
Get:12 http://ftp.cc.uoc.gr/mirrors/linux/ubuntu/packages xenial/main amd64 libxcomposite1 amd64 1:0.4.4-1 [7,714 B]
Get:13 http://ftp.cc.uoc.gr/mirrors/linux/ubuntu/packages xenial/main amd64 libxfixes3 amd64 1:5.0.1-2 [11.1 kB]
Get:14 http://ftp.cc.uoc.gr/mirrors/linux/ubuntu/packages xenial/main amd64 libxrender1 amd64 1:0.9.9-0ubuntu1 [18.5 kB]
Get:15 http://ftp.cc.uoc.gr/mirrors/linux/ubuntu/packages xenial/main amd64 libxcursor1 amd64 1:1.1.14-1 [22.8 kB]
Get:16 http://ftp.cc.uoc.gr/mirrors/linux/ubuntu/packages xenial/main amd64 libxdamage1 amd64 1:1.1.4-2 [6,946 B]
Get:17 http://ftp.cc.uoc.gr/mirrors/linux/ubuntu/packages xenial/main amd64 libxinerama1 amd64 2:1.1.3-1 [7,908 B]
Get:18 http://ftp.cc.uoc.gr/mirrors/linux/ubuntu/packages xenial/main amd64 libxshmfence1 amd64 1.2-1 [5,042 B]
Get:19 http://ftp.cc.uoc.gr/mirrors/linux/ubuntu/packages xenial/main amd64 x11-common all 1:7.7+13ubuntu3 [22.4 kB]
Get:20 http://ftp.cc.uoc.gr/mirrors/linux/ubuntu/packages xenial/main amd64 libxtst6 amd64 2:1.2.2-1 [14.1 kB]
Get:21 http://ftp.cc.uoc.gr/mirrors/linux/ubuntu/packages xenial/main amd64 libxxf86vm1 amd64 1:1.1.4-1 [10.6 kB]
Get:22 http://ftp.cc.uoc.gr/mirrors/linux/ubuntu/packages xenial-updates/main amd64 libnspr4 amd64 2:4.12-0ubuntu0.16.04.1 [112 kB]
Get:23 http://ftp.cc.uoc.gr/mirrors/linux/ubuntu/packages xenial-updates/main amd64 libnss3-nssdb all 2:3.23-0ubuntu0.16.04.1 [10.6 kB]
Get:24 http://ftp.cc.uoc.gr/mirrors/linux/ubuntu/packages xenial-updates/main amd64 libnss3 amd64 2:3.23-0ubuntu0.16.04.1 [1,144 kB]
Get:25 http://ftp.cc.uoc.gr/mirrors/linux/ubuntu/packages xenial/main amd64 ca-certificates-java all 20160321 [12.9 kB]
Get:26 http://ftp.cc.uoc.gr/mirrors/linux/ubuntu/packages xenial/main amd64 java-common all 0.56ubuntu2 [7,742 B]
Get:27 http://ftp.cc.uoc.gr/mirrors/linux/ubuntu/packages xenial/main amd64 libavahi-common-data amd64 0.6.32~rc+dfsg-1ubuntu2 [21.7 kB]
Get:28 http://ftp.cc.uoc.gr/mirrors/linux/ubuntu/packages xenial/main amd64 libavahi-common3 amd64 0.6.32~rc+dfsg-1ubuntu2 [21.6 kB]
Get:29 http://ftp.cc.uoc.gr/mirrors/linux/ubuntu/packages xenial/main amd64 libavahi-client3 amd64 0.6.32~rc+dfsg-1ubuntu2 [25.1 kB]
Get:30 http://ftp.cc.uoc.gr/mirrors/linux/ubuntu/packages xenial/main amd64 libcups2 amd64 2.1.3-4 [197 kB]
Get:31 http://ftp.cc.uoc.gr/mirrors/linux/ubuntu/packages xenial/main amd64 libjpeg8 amd64 8c-2ubuntu8 [2,194 B]
Get:32 http://ftp.cc.uoc.gr/mirrors/linux/ubuntu/packages xenial/main amd64 libxi6 amd64 2:1.7.6-1 [28.6 kB]
Get:33 http://ftp.cc.uoc.gr/mirrors/linux/ubuntu/packages xenial-updates/main amd64 openjdk-8-jre-headless amd64 8u91-b14-3ubuntu1~16.04.1 [26.9 MB]
Get:34 http://ftp.cc.uoc.gr/mirrors/linux/ubuntu/packages xenial/main amd64 libjbig0 amd64 2.1-3.1 [26.6 kB]
Get:35 http://ftp.cc.uoc.gr/mirrors/linux/ubuntu/packages xenial/main amd64 libtxc-dxtn-s2tc0 amd64 0~git20131104-1.1 [51.8 kB]
Get:36 http://ftp.cc.uoc.gr/mirrors/linux/ubuntu/packages xenial/main amd64 dbus-x11 amd64 1.10.6-1ubuntu3 [21.6 kB]
Get:37 http://ftp.cc.uoc.gr/mirrors/linux/ubuntu/packages xenial/main amd64 fonts-dejavu-extra all 2.35-1 [1,749 kB]
Get:38 http://ftp.cc.uoc.gr/mirrors/linux/ubuntu/packages xenial/main amd64 gconf2-common all 3.2.6-3ubuntu6 [21.0 kB]
Get:39 http://ftp.cc.uoc.gr/mirrors/linux/ubuntu/packages xenial/main amd64 libgconf-2-4 amd64 3.2.6-3ubuntu6 [84.6 kB]
Get:40 http://ftp.cc.uoc.gr/mirrors/linux/ubuntu/packages xenial/main amd64 gconf-service-backend amd64 3.2.6-3ubuntu6 [57.5 kB]
Get:41 http://ftp.cc.uoc.gr/mirrors/linux/ubuntu/packages xenial/main amd64 gconf-service amd64 3.2.6-3ubuntu6 [2,046 B]
Get:42 http://ftp.cc.uoc.gr/mirrors/linux/ubuntu/packages xenial/main amd64 gconf2 amd64 3.2.6-3ubuntu6 [65.8 kB]
Get:43 http://ftp.cc.uoc.gr/mirrors/linux/ubuntu/packages xenial/main amd64 hicolor-icon-theme all 0.15-0ubuntu1 [7,750 B]
```

Figure 1-6. *The number of packages that will be installed*

It will take some time to install all of the packages. Once this is done, you will have Java installed, as required by Logstash, in order to work properly.

Installing Logstash

Now we will move forward and install Logstash on our server. You can install the Logstash source from the following address: https://www.elastic.co/downloads/past-releases/logstash-2-4-1.

To begin simply, we will now explore how we can install Logstash from repositories on CentOS 7 and Ubuntu 16.04.1 LTS.

Installing Logstash on CentOS 7

First, we will download and install the public signing key (Figure 1-7). This is an important step to verify that the package is not corrupted or tampered with.

```
[vishne0@localhost ~]$ sudo rpm --import https://packages.elasticsearch.org/GPG-KEY-elasticsearch
```

```
[vishne0@localhost ~]$ sudo rpm --import https://packages.elasticsearch.org/GPG-KEY-elasticsearch
[vishne0@localhost ~]$
```

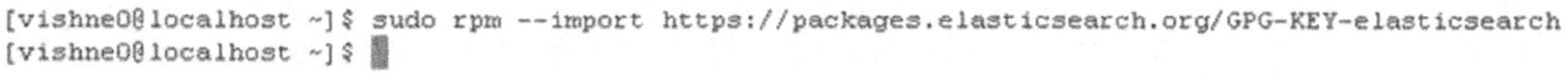

Figure 1-7. *Installing a public signing key*

Once complete, we will add the Logstash repository into our system, because the CentOS 7 default repository doesn't contain Logstash.

We will add it below in the /etc/yum.repos.d/ directory. We will use the standard text editor, nano or vi, from the command line, to create the new repository, as shown in Figure 1-8.

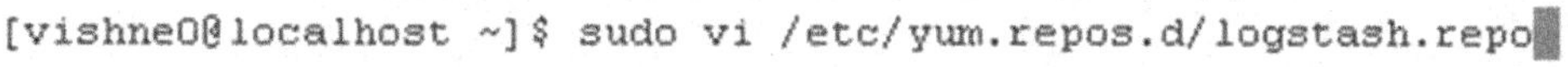

```
[vishne0@localhost ~]$ sudo vi /etc/yum.repos.d/logstash.repo
```

Figure 1-8. *Creating a repository using* vi

Let's name our repo logstash.repo. Issue the following command, to add the repository in your terminal window (see Figure 1-9).

```
[vishne0@localhost ~]$ sudo vi /etc/yum.repos.d/logstash.repo
Press i to insert text.
[logstash-2.4]
name=Logstash repository for 2.4.x packages
baseurl=https://packages.elastic.co/logstash/2.4/centos
gpgcheck=1
gpgkey=https://packages.elastic.co/GPG-KEY-elasticsearch
enabled=1
```

```
[logstash-2.4]
name=Logstash repository for 2.4.x packages
baseurl=https://packages.elastic.co/logstash/2.4/centos
gpgcheck=1
gpgkey=https://packages.elastic.co/GPG-KEY-elasticsearch
enabled=1
```

Figure 1-9. *Code for Logstash repo using* vi

Once you have added the repo, press ESC, then :wq inside the vi editor, to save it and exit (see Figure 1-10).

```
[logstash-2.4]
name=Logstash repository for 2.4.x packages
baseurl=https://packages.elastic.co/logstash/2.4/centos
gpgcheck=1
gpgkey=https://packages.elastic.co/GPG-KEY-elasticsearch
enabled=1

:wq
```

Figure 1-10. *Exiting* vi

If you are using nano, you have to issue the following commands in your terminal (see Figure 1-11):

```
[vishne0@centylog root]$ sudo nano /etc/yum.repos.d/logstash.repo
```

Figure 1-11. *Creating a Logstash repo file using* nano

To save the file in nano, press CTRL+X, and enter Y.

Now you are ready to install Logstash using yum (see Figure 1-12).

```
[vishne0@localhost ~]$ sudo yum install logstash
```

```
[vishne0@localhost ~]$ sudo yum install logstash
Loaded plugins: fastestmirror
logstash-2.4                                                                          |  951 B  00:00:00
logstash-2.4/primary                                                                  | 1.8 kB  00:00:01
Loading mirror speeds from cached hostfile
 * base: mirrors.linode.com
 * extras: mirrors.linode.com
 * updates: mirrors.linode.com
logstash-2.4                                                                                     1/1
Resolving Dependencies
--> Running transaction check
---> Package logstash.noarch 1:2.4.0-1 will be installed
--> Finished Dependency Resolution

Dependencies Resolved

================================================================================================================
 Package                      Arch              Version                 Repository             Size
================================================================================================================
Installing:
 logstash                     noarch            1:2.4.0-1               logstash-2.4           81 M

Transaction Summary
================================================================================================================
Install  1 Package

Total download size: 81 M
Installed size: 137 M
Is this ok [y/d/N]: y
Downloading packages:
logstash-2.4.0.noarch.rpm                                                             |  81 MB  00:00:15
Running transaction check
Running transaction test
Transaction test succeeded
Running transaction
  Installing : 1:logstash-2.4.0-1.noarch                                                         1/1
  Verifying  : 1:logstash-2.4.0-1.noarch                                                         1/1

Installed:
  logstash.noarch 1:2.4.0-1

Complete!
[vishne0@localhost ~]$
```

Figure 1-12. *Installing Logstash using* yum

Press Enter and then Y. Logstash is now installed on your server.

We will now check out the Logstash installation. By default, in CentOS 7, it will be installed in /opt. Enter the following command to change the directory to /opt/logstash (see Figure 1-13).

```
[vishne0@localhost ~]$ cd /opt/logstash/
```

```
[vishne0@localhost ~]$ cd /opt/logstash/
```

Figure 1-13. *Changing the directory to Logstash*

Now we will run Logstash, in order to check if it's working properly.

```
[vishne0@localhost logstash]$ sudo bin/logstash -e 'input { stdin { } } output { stdout {} }'
```

Press Enter, and then wait for few seconds, until you see a message on your screen, such as the one shown in Figure 1-14.

```
[vishne0@localhost ~]$ cd /opt/logstash/
[vishne0@localhost logstash]$ sudo bin/logstash -e 'input { stdin { } } output { stdout {} }'
Settings: Default pipeline workers: 2
Pipeline main started
```

Figure 1-14. *Running Logstash*

When you see the message that the Logstash start-up has completed, type in the following text and press Enter.

```
It Works!!!
```

You will see a message such as the following. It means that Logstash is working just fine (see Figure 1-15).

```
Pipeline main started
It works!!
2016-10-12T08:53:31.982Z localhost.localdomain It works!!
```

```
[vishne0@localhost ~]$ cd /opt/logstash/
[vishne0@localhost logstash]$ sudo bin/logstash -e 'input { stdin { } } output { stdout {} }'
Settings: Default pipeline workers: 2
Pipeline main started
It works!!
2016-10-12T08:53:31.982Z localhost.localdomain It works!!
```

Figure 1-15. *Logstash running successfully*

Now let's see what information Logstash is displaying. It shows us the date, timestamp, IP address or hostname (if you have configured one), and our message. In my case, the hostname is localhost.

There is one more thing that you may have noticed. It is a value 982Z, which is part of the timestamp; 982 is a fraction of a second; and Z represents UTC (a.k.a. Zulu), as Logstash normalizes all timestamps to UTC.

To stop running Logstash, press Ctrl+D.

Installing on Ubuntu 16.04.1 LTS

We installed OpenJDK 8 JRE earlier (see Figure 1-5). We will now install OpenJDK 8 JDK on Ubuntu 16.04.1 LTS. Open the terminal and issue the following commands (see Figure 1-16):

```
vishne0@snf-725572:~$ sudo apt-get install openjdk-8-jdk
```

```
vishne0@snf-725572:~$ sudo apt-get install openjdk-8-jdk
Reading package lists... Done
Building dependency tree
Reading state information... Done
The following additional packages will be installed:
  libice-dev libice6 libpthread-stubs0-dev libsm-dev libsm6 libx11-dev libx11-doc libxau-dev libxcb1-dev libxdmcp-dev libxt-dev libxt6 openjdk-8-jdk-headless
  x11proto-core-dev x11proto-input-dev x11proto-kb-dev xorg-sgml-doctools xtrans-dev
Suggested packages:
  libice-doc libsm-doc libxcb-doc libxt-doc openjdk-8-demo openjdk-8-source visualvm
The following NEW packages will be installed:
  libice-dev libice6 libpthread-stubs0-dev libsm-dev libsm6 libx11-dev libx11-doc libxau-dev libxcb1-dev libxdmcp-dev libxt-dev libxt6 openjdk-8-jdk
  openjdk-8-jdk-headless x11proto-core-dev x11proto-input-dev x11proto-kb-dev xorg-sgml-doctools xtrans-dev
0 upgraded, 19 newly installed, 0 to remove and 3 not upgraded.
Need to get 12.2 MB of archives.
After this operation, 58.8 MB of additional disk space will be used.
Do you want to continue? [Y/n] y
Get:1 http://ftp.cc.uoc.gr/mirrors/linux/ubuntu/packages xenial/main amd64 libice6 amd64 2:1.0.9-1 [39.2 kB]
Get:2 http://ftp.cc.uoc.gr/mirrors/linux/ubuntu/packages xenial/main amd64 libsm6 amd64 2:1.2.2-1 [15.8 kB]
Get:3 http://ftp.cc.uoc.gr/mirrors/linux/ubuntu/packages xenial/main amd64 xorg-sgml-doctools all 1:1.11-1 [12.9 kB]
Get:4 http://ftp.cc.uoc.gr/mirrors/linux/ubuntu/packages xenial/main amd64 x11proto-core-dev all 7.0.28-2ubuntu1 [254 kB]
Get:5 http://ftp.cc.uoc.gr/mirrors/linux/ubuntu/packages xenial/main amd64 libice-dev amd64 2:1.0.9-1 [44.9 kB]
Get:6 http://ftp.cc.uoc.gr/mirrors/linux/ubuntu/packages xenial/main amd64 libpthread-stubs0-dev amd64 0.3-4 [4,068 B]
Get:7 http://ftp.cc.uoc.gr/mirrors/linux/ubuntu/packages xenial/main amd64 libsm-dev amd64 2:1.2.2-1 [16.2 kB]
Get:8 http://ftp.cc.uoc.gr/mirrors/linux/ubuntu/packages xenial/main amd64 libxau-dev amd64 1:1.0.8-1 [11.1 kB]
Get:9 http://ftp.cc.uoc.gr/mirrors/linux/ubuntu/packages xenial/main amd64 libxdmcp-dev amd64 1:1.1.2-1.1 [25.1 kB]
Get:10 http://ftp.cc.uoc.gr/mirrors/linux/ubuntu/packages xenial/main amd64 x11proto-input-dev all 2.3.1-1 [118 kB]
Get:11 http://ftp.cc.uoc.gr/mirrors/linux/ubuntu/packages xenial/main amd64 x11proto-kb-dev all 1.0.7-0ubuntu1 [224 kB]
Get:12 http://ftp.cc.uoc.gr/mirrors/linux/ubuntu/packages xenial/main amd64 xtrans-dev all 1.3.5-1 [70.5 kB]
Get:13 http://ftp.cc.uoc.gr/mirrors/linux/ubuntu/packages xenial/main amd64 libxcb1-dev amd64 1.11.1-1ubuntu1 [74.2 kB]
Get:14 http://ftp.cc.uoc.gr/mirrors/linux/ubuntu/packages xenial/main amd64 libx11-dev amd64 2:1.6.3-1ubuntu2 [642 kB]
Get:15 http://ftp.cc.uoc.gr/mirrors/linux/ubuntu/packages xenial/main amd64 libx11-doc all 2:1.6.3-1ubuntu2 [1,465 kB]
Get:16 http://ftp.cc.uoc.gr/mirrors/linux/ubuntu/packages xenial/main amd64 libxt6 amd64 1:1.1.5-0ubuntu1 [160 kB]
Get:17 http://ftp.cc.uoc.gr/mirrors/linux/ubuntu/packages xenial/main amd64 libxt-dev amd64 1:1.1.5-0ubuntu1 [394 kB]
Get:18 http://ftp.cc.uoc.gr/mirrors/linux/ubuntu/packages xenial-updates/main amd64 openjdk-8-jdk-headless amd64 8u91-b14-3ubuntu1~16.04.1 [8,166 kB]
Get:19 http://ftp.cc.uoc.gr/mirrors/linux/ubuntu/packages xenial-updates/main amd64 openjdk-8-jdk amd64 8u91-b14-3ubuntu1~16.04.1 [430 kB]
Fetched 12.2 MB in 4s (2,770 kB/s)
Selecting previously unselected package libice6:amd64.
(Reading database ... 61516 files and directories currently installed.)
Preparing to unpack .../libice6_2%3a1.0.9-1_amd64.deb ...
Unpacking libice6:amd64 (2:1.0.9-1) ...
Selecting previously unselected package libsm6:amd64.
Preparing to unpack .../libsm6_2%3a1.2.2-1_amd64.deb ...
Unpacking libsm6:amd64 (2:1.2.2-1) ...
Selecting previously unselected package xorg-sgml-doctools.
```

Figure 1-16. *Installing OpenJDK 8 JDK*

Press Enter and then Y, apt-get will install all the dependencies required by the package.

Now we will install Logstash on our Ubuntu server. First, we will install the public signing key with following commands:

```
vishne0@snf-725572:~$ sudo wget -qO - https://packages.elastic.co/GPG-KEY-elasticsearch |
sudo apt-key add -
```

Now we add the Logstash repository to the /etc/apt/source.list.d/ file, with the following commands:

```
vishne0@snf-725572:~$ echo "deb http://packages.elastic.co/logstash/2.4/debian stable main"
| sudo tee -a /etc/apt/sources.list.d/logstash.list
```

Next, we will update our repository with the following command (see Figure 1-17):

```
vishneo@:~$ sudo apt-get update
```

```
vishne0@snf-725572:~$ sudo apt-get update
Hit:1 http://ftp.cc.uoc.gr/mirrors/linux/ubuntu/packages xenial InRelease
Hit:2 http://ftp.cc.uoc.gr/mirrors/linux/ubuntu/packages xenial-updates InRelease
Hit:3 http://ftp.cc.uoc.gr/mirrors/linux/ubuntu/packages xenial-backports InRelease
Hit:4 http://security.ubuntu.com/ubuntu xenial-security InRelease
Ign:5 http://packages.elastic.co/logstash/2.4/debian stable InRelease
Get:6 http://packages.elastic.co/logstash/2.4/debian stable Release [3,301 B]
Get:7 http://packages.elastic.co/logstash/2.4/debian stable Release.gpg [490 B]
Get:8 http://packages.elastic.co/logstash/2.4/debian stable/main amd64 Packages [496 B]
Get:9 http://packages.elastic.co/logstash/2.4/debian stable/main i386 Packages [496 B]
Fetched 4,783 B in 2s (1,687 B/s)
Reading package lists... Done
W: http://packages.elastic.co/logstash/2.4/debian/dists/stable/Release.gpg: Signature by key 46095ACC8548582C1A2699A9D27D666CD88E42B4 uses weak digest algorithm (SHA1)
vishne0@snf-725572:~$ ▊
```

Figure 1-17. *Updating repository using* apt-get *update*

Once it has been updated, we will install Logstash, using the following command (see Figure 1-18):

```
vishne0@snf-725572:~$ sudo apt-get install logstash
```

```
vishne0@snf-725572:~$ sudo apt-get install logstash
Reading package lists... Done
Building dependency tree
Reading state information... Done
The following NEW packages will be installed:
  logstash
0 upgraded, 1 newly installed, 0 to remove and 3 not upgraded.
Need to get 84.8 MB of archives.
After this operation, 143 MB of additional disk space will be used.
Get:1 http://packages.elastic.co/logstash/2.4/debian stable/main amd64 logstash all 1:2.4.0-1 [84.8 MB]
Fetched 84.8 MB in 13s (6,142 kB/s)
Selecting previously unselected package logstash.
(Reading database ... 63079 files and directories currently installed.)
Preparing to unpack .../logstash_1%3a2.4.0-1_all.deb ...
Unpacking logstash (1:2.4.0-1) ...
Processing triggers for systemd (229-4ubuntu10) ...
Processing triggers for ureadahead (0.100.0-19) ...
Setting up logstash (1:2.4.0-1) ...
Processing triggers for systemd (229-4ubuntu10) ...
Processing triggers for ureadahead (0.100.0-19) ...
vishne0@snf-725572:~$ 
```

Figure 1-18. *Installing Logstash on Ubuntu 16.04.1 LTS*

The command will install Logstash in the /opt directory. Run the following command to go to the logstash/ directory (see Figure 1-19).

```
vishne0@snf-725572:/$ cd /opt/logstash/
```

```
vishne0@snf-725572:/$ cd /opt/logstash/
vishne0@snf-725572:/opt/logstash$ 
```

Figure 1-19. *Changing the directory to /opt/logstash/bin*

Now we are inside the bin directory. Enter the following command to test your installation on Ubuntu. We will run this command. Once you see that Pipeline main has started, type "It Works!!!".

```
vishne0@snf-725572:/opt/logstash$ sudo bin/logstash -e 'input { stdin { } }
output { stdout {} }'
```

```
It Works!!!
2016-10-12T09:56:58.057Z snf-725572 IIt Works!!!
```

As you can see, it is working just fine on Ubuntu too. As previously noted, here you are seeing the date, timestamp, IP address or hostname (if you have configured one), and our message. In my case, the hostname is snf-725572.

There is one more thing you that may have noticed. It is a value of 851Z. It is part of the timestamp. 851 is a fraction of a second, and Z represents UTC (a.k.a. Zulu), as Logstash normalizes all timestamps to UTC.

To stop running Logstash, press Ctrl+D.

Logstash CLI Flags

It's always a good idea to familiarize yourself with the options an application provides. The following is a listing of all of the CLI flags that Logstash provides (see Table 1-1). You can use the --help option to see all this information.

```
vishneO@snf-725572:/opt/logstash$ sudo bin/logstash --help
Usage:
    /bin/logstash agent [OPTIONS]
```

Table 1-1. *Logstash CLI Flags*

Options	Summary
-f, --config CONFIG_PATH	Load the Logstash config from a specific file or directory. If a directory is given, all of the files in that directory will be concatenated in lexicographical order and then parsed as a single config file. You can also specify wildcards (globs), and any matched files will be loaded in the order described previously.
-e CONFIG_STRING	Use the given string as the configuration data. It has the same syntax as the config file. If no input is specified, then the following is used as the default input: "input { stdin { type => stdin } }". If no output is specified, the following is used as the default output: "output { stdout { codec => rubydebug } }". If you wish to use both defaults, use the empty string for the -e flag (default: "").
-w, --filterworkers COUNT	Sets the number of filter workers to run. (default: 0)
-l, --log FILE	Writes Logstash internal logs to the given file. Without this flag, Logstash will transmit logs to standard output.
-v	Increases verbosity of Logstash internal logs. Specifying this once will show "informational" logs. Specifying it twice will show "debug" logs. This flag is deprecated. You should use --verbose or --debug instead.
--quiet	Quieter Logstash logging. This causes only errors to be transmitted.
--verbose	More verbose logging. This causes "info"-level logs to be transmitted.
--debug	Most verbose logging. This causes "debug"-level logs to be transmitted.
-V, --version	Emit the version of Logstash and its friends and then exit.
-p, --pluginpath PATH	A path to where plug-ins can be found. This flag can be issued multiple times to include multiple paths. Plug-ins are expected to be in a specific directory hierarchy: 'PATH/logstash/TYPE/NAME.rb' where TYPE is 'inputs', 'filters', 'outputs', or 'codecs' and NAME is the name of the plug-in.
-t, --configtest	Check configuration for valid syntax and then exit.
--[no-]allow-unsafe-shutdown	Force Logstash to exit during shutdown, even if there are still in-process events in memory. By default, Logstash will refuse to quit until all received events have been pushed to the outputs. (default: false)
-h, --help	print help

Logstash Configuration

Now that Logstash is installed and you have checked the CLI flags, it is time to configure it. We will do a very simple configuration here.

Create and save the file in the Logstash configuration directory in /etc/logstash/conf.d using vi or nano.

```
[vishne0@localhost logstash]$ sudo vi /etc/logstash/conf.d/logstash-sample.conf
```

In our first sample, we will have a simple input and output, as follows:

```
## Sample Logstash Config
input {
  stdin {}
}
output {
  stdout {}
}
```

We will now run Logstash, to see if this file works. Change the directory to /opt/logstash and issue the following command:

```
[vishne0@localhost logstash]$ sudo bin/logstash -f /etc/logstash/conf.d/logstash-sample.conf
```

Press Enter, then type Config Test. Press Enter again, and you will see the following output:

```
Pipeline main started
Config Test
2016-10-12T09:05:01.470Z localhost.localdomain Config Test
```

As you can see, the correct output is displayed, so our sample config file is working just fine, as shown in Figure 1-20.

```
[vishne0@localhost logstash]$ sudo bin/logstash -f /etc/logstash/conf.d/logstash-sample.conf
Settings: Default pipeline workers: 2
Pipeline main started
Config Test
2016-10-12T09:05:01.470Z localhost.localdomain Config Test
```

Figure 1-20. *Running Logstash using our sample configuration*

Logstash Logs

By default, Logstash stores all the logs in /var/log/logstash. You will not see any logs for now but will when in later chapters we configure Logstash to parse log files.

Upgrading Logstash

As we are using CentOS 7 and Ubuntu 16.04.1 LTS servers for our setup, we will always upgrade Logstash using such package managers as yum and apt. Before upgrading Logstash, shut down the Logstash pipeline

```
[vishne0@localhost /]$ sudo service logstash stop

On CentOS 7 server
[vishne0@localhost /]$ sudo yum update logstash

On Ubuntu 16.04.1 LTS
[vishne0@localhost /]$ sudo apt-get upgrade logstash
```

Once Logstash is upgraded, you can test your configuration files by changing the directory to /opt/logstash and running the following:

```
[vishne0@localhost logstash]$ sudo bin/logstash -f /etc/logstash/conf.d/
nameofconfigurationfile.conf
```

If any updates appear in your configuration file, then do the updates. Once done, start Logstash.

```
[vishne0@localhost logstash]$ sudo service logstash start
```

Summary

In this chapter, we tested our Logstash installation on CentOS 7 and Ubuntu 16.04.1 LTS. I have also introduced you to what Logstash can be used for and how to do the following:

- Install Logstash
- Configure Logstash
- Run Logstash using a simple configuration on our server

In next chapters, you will learn more about how to install Elasticsearch and Kibana and how to configure them in order to have our setup ready.

■ ■ ■

## CHAPTER 2

Getting Started with Elasticsearch

Now that we've installed Logstash, we will move forward and install and configure Elasticsearch. Before we do this, let me explain first a little bit more about Elasticsearch.

What Is Elasticsearch?

Elasticsearch, developed by Shay Banon, is written in Java. It is open source and based on Apache Lucene, under an Apache license.

So what does Elasticsearch really do? Elasticsearch is a scalable full-text search and analytics engine. It works with large data and lets you store and perform searches on it. Because Elasticsearch is based on Apache Lucene, it does incremental indexing, which makes Elasticsearch lighting fast.

For simplicity's sake, take, for example, a big e-commercial web site such as Amazon.com. It contains millions of products in a large number of categories. Elasticsearch comes in handy if, say, one manages the Amazon web site and wants to search for products that are trending on the store or one wants to search the entire Amazon catalog for specific products that are out of stock in all categories. Elasticsearch can do this and a lot more, which you will discover in later chapters.

Installing Elasticsearch on CentOS 7

Elasticsearch requires Java to be installed. As we already installed Java in Chapter 1, we now just have to check the Java installation on CentOS 7.

Log into the server using SSH, and if you are logged in as root, you have to add a user and add it to the sudoers list. Issue the following commands to add a user (see Figure 2-1):

```
[root@localhost ~]# adduser vishne0
```

```
[root@localhost ~]# adduser Vishne0
[root@localhost ~]# passwd Vishne0
Changing password for user Vishne0.
New password:
Retype new password:
passwd: all authentication tokens updated successfully.
[root@localhost ~]#
```

Figure 2-1. *Issuing the commands to add a user*

© Vishal Sharma 2016
V. Sharma, *Beginning Elastic Stack*, DOI 10.1007/978-1-4842-1694-1_2

Give it a password, as follows:

```
[root@localhost ~]# passwd vishne0
```

Once complete, log out and log back in as user.Remember to add the user to the sudoers file. Please refer to Chapter 1 for how to add add a user to the sudoers file.

Now we will check the Java version. Issue the following commands (see Figure 2-2):

```
[vishne0@localhost /]$ java -version
openjdk version "1.8.0_102"
OpenJDK Runtime Environment (build 1.8.0_102-b14)
OpenJDK 64-Bit Server VM (build 25.102-b14, mixed mode)
```

```
[vishne0@localhost /]$ java -version
openjdk version "1.8.0_102"
OpenJDK Runtime Environment (build 1.8.0_102-b14)
OpenJDK 64-Bit Server VM (build 25.102-b14, mixed mode)
[vishne0@localhost /]$
```

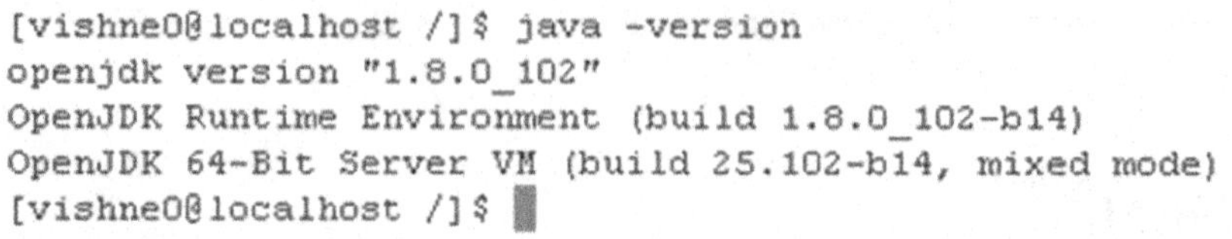

Figure 2-2. *Checking the Java version*

Now that we have installed Java (see Figure 2-2), we will move on and install Elasticsearch on CentOS 7.

We will first download and install the public signing key, to make sure that the package is not corrupt or hasn't been tampered with.

```
[vishne0@localhost /]$ sudo rpm --import https://packages.elastic.co/GPG-KEY-elasticsearch
```

Now we will add the repository in our system and install Elasticsearch. Let's create the elasticsearch. repo (see Figure 2-3).

```
[vishne0@centylog ]$ sudo vi /etc/yum.repos.d/elasticsearch.repo
```

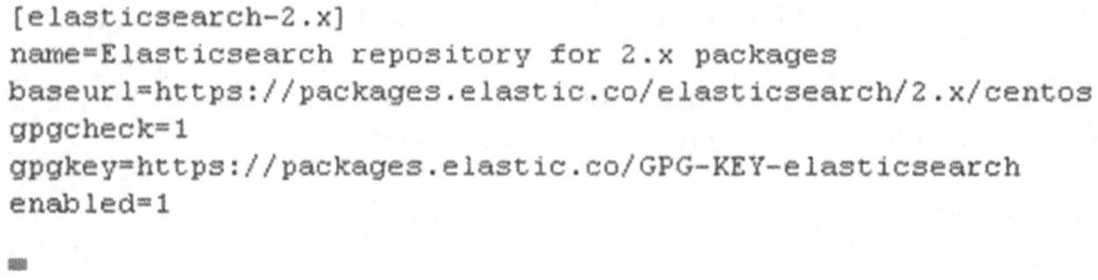

```
[elasticsearch-2.x]
name=Elasticsearch repository for 2.x packages
baseurl=https://packages.elastic.co/elasticsearch/2.x/centos
gpgcheck=1
gpgkey=https://packages.elastic.co/GPG-KEY-elasticsearch
enabled=1
```

Figure 2-3. *Creating* elasticsearch.repo

Press i to enter the following code:

```
[elasticsearch-2.x]
name=Elasticsearch repository for 2.x packages
baseurl=https://packages.elastic.co/elasticsearch/2.x/centos
gpgcheck=1
gpgkey=https://packages.elastic.co/GPG-KEY-elasticsearch
enabled=1
```

Press the Esc key and then enter :wq to save and exit vi. Now that our repository is ready to use, let's install Elasticsearch.

Issue the following command to install Elasticsearch (Figure 2-4):

```
[vishne0@localhost /]$ sudo yum install elasticsearch
```

```
[vishne0@localhost /]$ sudo yum install elasticsearch
Loaded plugins: fastestmirror
elasticsearch-2.x                                                          | 2.9 kB  00:00:00
elasticsearch-2.x/primary_db                                               | 7.7 kB  00:00:01
Loading mirror speeds from cached hostfile
 * base: mirrors.linode.com
 * extras: mirrors.linode.com
 * updates: mirrors.linode.com
Resolving Dependencies
--> Running transaction check
---> Package elasticsearch.noarch 0:2.4.1-1 will be installed
--> Finished Dependency Resolution

Dependencies Resolved

=================================================================================================
 Package            Arch           Version          Repository             Size
=================================================================================================
Installing:
 elasticsearch      noarch         2.4.1-1          elasticsearch-2.x      26 M

Transaction Summary
=================================================================================================
Install  1 Package

Total download size: 26 M
Installed size: 29 M
Is this ok [y/d/N]: y
Downloading packages:
elasticsearch-2.4.1.rpm                                                    |  26 MB  00:00:11
Running transaction check
Running transaction test
Transaction test succeeded
Running transaction
Creating elasticsearch group... OK
Creating elasticsearch user... OK
  Installing : elasticsearch-2.4.1-1.noarch                                                1/1
### NOT starting on installation, please execute the following statements to configure elasticsearch service to start automatically using systemd
 sudo systemctl daemon-reload
 sudo systemctl enable elasticsearch.service
### You can start elasticsearch service by executing
 sudo systemctl start elasticsearch.service
  Verifying  : elasticsearch-2.4.1-1.noarch                                                1/1
```

Figure 2-4. *Installing Elasticsearch using* yum

Elasticsearch is installed, as you can see in Figure 2-4. Now we will add Elasticsearch to init scripts, so that it will start while CentOS 7 is booting (see Figure 2-5).

```
[vishne0@localhost /]$ sudo systemctl enable elasticsearch.service
[sudo] password for vishne0:
Created symlink from /etc/systemd/system/multi-user.target.wants/elasticsearch.service to /
usr/lib/systemd/system/elasticsearch.service.
```

```
[vishne0@localhost /]$ sudo systemctl enable elasticsearch.service
[sudo] password for vishne0:
Created symlink from /etc/systemd/system/multi-user.target.wants/elasticsearch.service to /usr/lib/systemd/system/elasticsearch.service.
[vishne0@localhost /]$ ▮
```

Figure 2-5. *Adding Elasticsearch to the* init *scripts*

Installing Elasticsearch on Ubuntu 16.04.1 LTS

Open the console, to check if you have Java installed on your server (see Figure 2-6).

```
vishne0@snf-725572:/$ java -version
openjdk version "1.8.0_91"
OpenJDK Runtime Environment (build 1.8.0_91-8u91-b14-3ubuntu1~16.04.1-b14)
OpenJDK 64-Bit Server VM (build 25.91-b14, mixed mode)
```

```
vishne0@snf-725572:/$ java -version
openjdk version "1.8.0_91"
OpenJDK Runtime Environment (build 1.8.0_91-8u91-b14-3ubuntu1~16.04.1-b14)
OpenJDK 64-Bit Server VM (build 25.91-b14, mixed mode)
```

Figure 2-6. *Checking the Java version installed*

As you can see here, Java is already installed, so we can now move ahead and install Elasticsearch. Let's first download and install the public signing key.

```
vishne0@snf-725572:/$ wget -qO - https://packages.elastic.co/GPG-KEY-elasticsearch | sudo
apt-key add -
```

Now let's add the Elasticsearch repository to our system (Figure 2-7).

```
vishne0@snf-725572:/$ echo "deb https://packages.elastic.co/elasticsearch/2.x/debian stable
main" | sudo tee -a /etc/apt/sources.list.d/elasticsearch-2.x.list
```

```
vishne0@snf-725572:/$ echo "deb https://packages.elastic.co/elasticsearch/2.x/debian stable main" | sudo tee -a /etc/apt/sources.list.d/elasticsearch-2.x.list
deb https://packages.elastic.co/elasticsearch/2.x/debian stable main
vishne0@snf-725572:/$
```

Figure 2-7. *Adding Elasticsearch to the repository*

Now that the repository includes Elasticsearch, issue the following command (see Figure 2-8):

```
vishne0@snf-725572:/$ sudo apt-get update && sudo apt-get install elasticsearch
```

```
vishne0@snf-725572:/$ sudo apt-get update && sudo apt-get install elasticsearch
[sudo] password for vishne0:
Hit:1 http://ftp.cc.uoc.gr/mirrors/linux/ubuntu/packages xenial InRelease
Get:2 http://ftp.cc.uoc.gr/mirrors/linux/ubuntu/packages xenial-updates InRelease [95.7 kB]
Hit:3 http://ftp.cc.uoc.gr/mirrors/linux/ubuntu/packages xenial-backports InRelease
Get:4 http://security.ubuntu.com/ubuntu xenial-security InRelease [94.5 kB]
Get:5 http://ftp.cc.uoc.gr/mirrors/linux/ubuntu/packages xenial-updates/main amd64 Packages [402 kB]
Get:6 http://ftp.cc.uoc.gr/mirrors/linux/ubuntu/packages xenial-updates/main i386 Packages [397 kB]
Get:7 http://ftp.cc.uoc.gr/mirrors/linux/ubuntu/packages xenial-updates/main Translation-en [153 kB]
Get:8 http://ftp.cc.uoc.gr/mirrors/linux/ubuntu/packages xenial-updates/universe amd64 Packages [336 kB]
Ign:9 http://packages.elastic.co/logstash/2.4/debian stable InRelease
Get:10 http://ftp.cc.uoc.gr/mirrors/linux/ubuntu/packages xenial-updates/universe i386 Packages [333 kB]
Hit:11 http://packages.elastic.co/logstash/2.4/debian stable Release
Get:12 http://ftp.cc.uoc.gr/mirrors/linux/ubuntu/packages xenial-updates/universe Translation-en [117 kB]
Ign:14 https://packages.elastic.co/elasticsearch/2.x/debian stable InRelease
Get:15 https://packages.elastic.co/elasticsearch/2.x/debian stable Release [1,763 B]
Get:16 https://packages.elastic.co/elasticsearch/2.x/debian stable Release.gpg [473 B]
Get:17 https://packages.elastic.co/elasticsearch/2.x/debian stable/main amd64 Packages [2,576 B]
Fetched 1,932 kB in 3s (602 kB/s)
Reading package lists... Done
W: http://packages.elastic.co/logstash/2.4/debian/dists/stable/Release.gpg: Signature by key 46095ACC8548582C1A2699A9D27D666CD88E42B4 uses weak digest algorithm (SHA1)
Reading package lists... Done
Building dependency tree
Reading state information... Done
The following NEW packages will be installed:
  elasticsearch
0 upgraded, 1 newly installed, 0 to remove and 16 not upgraded.
Need to get 27.3 MB of archives.
After this operation, 30.6 MB of additional disk space will be used.
Get:1 https://packages.elastic.co/elasticsearch/2.x/debian stable/main amd64 elasticsearch all 2.4.1 [27.3 MB]
Fetched 27.3 MB in 14s (1,924 kB/s)
Selecting previously unselected package elasticsearch.
(Reading database ... 75529 files and directories currently installed.)
Preparing to unpack .../elasticsearch_2.4.1_all.deb ...
Creating elasticsearch group... OK
Creating elasticsearch user... OK
Unpacking elasticsearch (2.4.1) ...
Processing triggers for systemd (229-4ubuntu10) ...
Processing triggers for ureadahead (0.100.0-19) ...
Setting up elasticsearch (2.4.1) ...
Processing triggers for systemd (229-4ubuntu10) ...
Processing triggers for ureadahead (0.100.0-19)
```

Figure 2-8. *Installing Elasticsearch*

As seen in Figure 2-8, we first updated our repository and then installed Elasticsearch. Elasticsearch is now installed. Next, we will add it to init scripts, to start it while the Ubuntu operating system (OS) is booting (see Figure 2-9).

```
vishne0@snf-725572:/$ sudo update-rc.d elasticsearch defaults
```

```
vishne0@snf-725572:/$ sudo update-rc.d elasticsearch defaults
vishne0@snf-725572:/$
```

Figure 2-9. *Adding Elasticsearch to the* init *script*

Elasticsearch is now installed on our Ubuntu 16.04.1 LTS service, and we have also added it to our init scripts. In next section, we will configure Elasticsearch.

Now that Elasticsearch is installed, we can proceed with configuring it.

Configuring Elasticsearch on CentOS 7

When we installed Elasticsearch, it created the configuration directory in /etc/elasticsearch. In that directory, we have two configuration files: elasticsearch.yml and logging.yml.

> elasticsearch.yml: This file contains all the server settings that we need.

> logging.yml: This file contains all the settings required for logging.

First, we will examine the elasticsearch.yml configuration file. To open the configuration file in our terminal window, we will use the following command (see Figure 2-10):

```
[vishne0@localhost /]$ sudo vi /etc/elasticsearch/elasticsearch.yml or if you are using nano
[vishne0@localhost /]$ sudo nano /etc/elasticsearch/elasticsearch.yml
```

```
# ======================= Elasticsearch Configuration ==========================
#
# NOTE: Elasticsearch comes with reasonable defaults for most settings.
#       Before you set out to tweak and tune the configuration, make sure you
#       understand what are you trying to accomplish and the consequences.
#
# The primary way of configuring a node is via this file. This template lists
# the most important settings you may want to configure for a production cluster.
#
# Please see the documentation for further information on configuration options:
# <http://www.elastic.co/guide/en/elasticsearch/reference/current/setup-configuration.html>
#
# ---------------------------------- Cluster -----------------------------------
#
# Use a descriptive name for your cluster:
#
# cluster.name: my-application
#
# ------------------------------------ Node ------------------------------------
#
# Use a descriptive name for the node:
#
# node.name: node-1
#
# Add custom attributes to the node:
#
# node.rack: r1
#
# ----------------------------------- Paths ------------------------------------
#
# Path to directory where to store the data (separate multiple locations by comma):
#
# path.data: /path/to/data
#
# Path to log files:
#
# path.logs: /path/to/logs
#
# ----------------------------------- Memory -----------------------------------
#
# Lock the memory on startup:
#
# bootstrap.memory_lock: true
"/etc/elasticsearch/elasticsearch.yml" 94L, 3192C
```

Figure 2-10. *Elasticsearch configuration file*

Press Enter and our configuration file will open.

As shown in Figure 2-10, when we open the configuration file, we have to focus our attention on two variables: cluster.name and node.name as you can configure Elasticsearch service as Cluster as well, where multiple nodes cooperate to store,index and search data.

> cluster.name: This is the cluster that will be associated with the node.

> node.name: This is the server name. Here you can specify the name or, if you have hostname, it will pick the hostname automatically.

cluster.name also helps Elasticsearch to discover the clusters automatically and associate them with the nodes.

Now we will change the values of cluster.name and node.name in our configuration file.

In my case, I make cluster.name = Cluster 1 and node.name = centylog, as seen in Figure 2-11.

```
# Use a descriptive name for your cluster:
#
 cluster.name: Cluster 1
#
# -------------------------------------- Node --------------------------------------
#
# Use a descriptive name for the node:
#
 node.name: centylog
#
```

Figure 2-11. *Configuring Elasticsearch*

Elasticsearch works in master/slave mode. Master servers keep track of the health of cluster servers, and slave servers are where data is stored.

For now, we will make a single server act as both master and slave, to test our Elasticsearch installation and configuration.

Configuring Network Settings

We will now go to the network section and configure the values there. In the network section, we will uncomment network.host and set the value there, as we want to test it on localhost.

network.host: localhost

Now let's uncomment http.port and set it to the default value of port 9200 (see Figure 2-12).

http.port: 9200

```
# Set the bind address to a specific IP (IPv4 or IPv6):
#
 network.host: localhost
#
# Set a custom port for HTTP:
#
 http.port: 9200
#
```

Figure 2-12. *Elasticsearch configuration*

Save the configuration file, and we will now test our installation. To do so, we must start Elasticsearch, so that it can read the configuration file (see Figure 2-13).

```
[vishne0@localhost /]$ sudo service elasticsearch restart
[sudo] password for vishne0:
Restarting elasticsearch (via systemctl):                [  OK  ]
```

```
[vishne0@localhost /]$ sudo service elasticsearch restart
[sudo] password for vishne0:
Restarting elasticsearch (via systemctl):              [  OK  ]
[vishne0@localhost /]$ ▮
```

Figure 2-13. *Restarting the Elasticsearch service*

To test our installation to see if it is running on port 9200, we will run the following commands (see Figure 2-14):

```
[vishne0@localhost /]$ curl -X GET 'http://localhost:9200'  and press enter. You should see
the output similar to below
[vishne0@localhost /]$ curl -X GET 'http://localhost:9200'
{
  "name" : "centylog",
  "cluster_name" : "Cluster 1",
  "cluster_uuid" : "gx6mNmDRQDekvCQ92VWwMQ",
  "version" : {
    "number" : "2.4.1",
    "build_hash" : "c67dc32e24162035d18d6fe1e952c4cbcbe79d16",
    "build_timestamp" : "2016-09-27T18:57:55Z",
    "build_snapshot" : false,
    "lucene_version" : "5.5.2"
  },
  "tagline" : "You Know, for Search"
}
```

```
[vishne0@localhost /]$ sudo service elasticsearch restart
[sudo] password for vishne0:
Restarting elasticsearch (via systemctl):              [  OK  ]
[vishne0@localhost /]$ curl -X GET 'http://localhost:9200'
{
  "name" : "centylog",
  "cluster_name" : "Cluster 1",
  "cluster_uuid" : "gx6mNmDRQDekvCQ92VWwMQ",
  "version" : {
    "number" : "2.4.1",
    "build_hash" : "c67dc32e24162035d18d6fe1e952c4cbcbe79d16",
    "build_timestamp" : "2016-09-27T18:57:55Z",
    "build_snapshot" : false,
    "lucene_version" : "5.5.2"
  },
  "tagline" : "You Know, for Search"
}
[vishne0@localhost /]$ ▮
```

Figure 2-14. *Checking the Elasticsearch installation*

The output shown in the figure means that Elasticsearch is working properly.

Configuring Elasticsearch on Ubuntu 16.04.1 LTS

Now let's configure Elasticsearch. You can find the configuration files in /etc/elasticsearch. We will edit elasticsearch.yml, as we have done previously on CentOS 7. The only four values that have to be changed are as follows:

> cluster.name: Uncomment it and put the cluster name here. In my case, I have set the name as Cluster 1.
>
> node.name: Uncomment it and put the hostname of your machine here.
>
> node.name: ubulog
>
> network.host: localhost. It should be localhost for now, as we are testing it.
>
> http.port: 9200. This is the default port.

After making changes in the configuration file, we will test our installation on Ubuntu, as we have done previously on CentOS 7. We have to start the Elasticsearch service on Ubuntu before we can test our configuration (see Figure 2-15).

```
vishne0@snf-725572:/$ sudo service elasticsearch start
```

```
vishne0@snf-725572:/$ curl -X GET 'http://localhost:9200'
{
  "name" : "ubulog",
  "cluster_name" : "Cluster 1",
  "cluster_uuid" : "am7ffDsNSCuae8onHfwy7w",
  "version" : {
    "number" : "2.4.1",
    "build_hash" : "c67dc32e24162035d18d6fe1e952c4cbcbe79d16",
    "build_timestamp" : "2016-09-27T18:57:55Z",
    "build_snapshot" : false,
    "lucene_version" : "5.5.2"
  },
  "tagline" : "You Know, for Search"
}
```

Figure 2-15. *Testing Elasticsearch*

Now let's test our installation and configuration by running the following commands, as we have done previously for CentOS 7 (see Figure 2-16).

```
vishne0@snf-725572:/$ curl -X GET 'http://localhost:9200'
{
  "name" : "ubulog",
  "cluster_name" : "Cluster 1",
```

25

```
  "cluster_uuid" : "am7ffDsNSCuae8onHfwy7w",
  "version" : {
    "number" : "2.4.1",
    "build_hash" : "c67dc32e24162035d18d6fe1e952c4cbcbe79d16",
    "build_timestamp" : "2016-09-27T18:57:55Z",
    "build_snapshot" : false,
    "lucene_version" : "5.5.2"
  },
  "tagline" : "You Know, for Search"
}
```

As you can see in the Figure 2-16, our Elasticsearch installation and configuration are working just fine on our Ubuntu 16.04.1 machine.

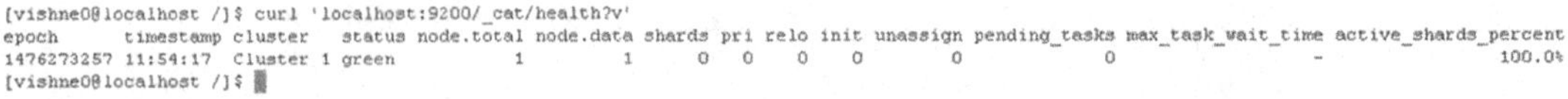

Figure 2-16. Showing Elasticsearch cluster health

There are few more things we can do. We can check cluster health by issuing the following command:

```
[vishne0@localhost /]$ curl 'localhost:9200/_cat/health?v'
epoch       timestamp cluster   status node.total node.data shards pri relo init unassign
pending_tasks max_task_wait_time active_shards_percent
1476273257 11:54:17  Cluster 1
green           1          1      0  0  0  0      0          0              -
                100.0%
```

As shown in Figure 2-16, the cluster health is showing up in green.

Creating an Index

We can create an index by issuing the following command:

```
[vishne0@localhost /]$ curl -XPUT 'localhost:9200/sampleindex?pretty'
{
  "acknowledged" : true
}
```

Let's check if the index is in list.

```
[vishne0@localhost /]$ curl 'localhost:9200/_cat/indices?v'
health status index       pri rep docs.count docs.deleted store.size pri.store.size
yellow open   sampleindex  5   1          0            0       650b           650b
```

As we can see in Figure 2-17, the sample index we have created is showing in the list.

```
[vishne0@localhost /]$ curl -XPUT 'localhost:9200/sampleindex?pretty'
{
  "acknowledged" : true
}
[vishne0@localhost /]$ curl 'localhost:9200/_cat/indices?v'
health status index          pri rep docs.count docs.deleted store.size pri.store.size
yellow open    sampleindex     5   1          0            0       650b           650b
[vishne0@localhost /]$
```

Figure 2-17. *The Elasticsearch index list*

Deleting an Index

We can delete an index (Figure 2-18) by running the following command:

```
[vishne0@localhost /]$ curl -XDELETE 'localhost:9200/sampleindex?pretty'
{
  "acknowledged" : true
}
```

```
[vishne0@localhost /]$ curl -XDELETE 'localhost:9200/sampleindex?pretty'
{
  "acknowledged" : true
}
```

Figure 2-18. *Deleting an index from Elasticsearch*

As shown in Figure 2-18, we have deleted the sample index successfully.

Upgrading Elasticsearch

As we are using CentOS 7 and Ubuntu 16.04.1 LTS distributions for our setup, we will be using the package management provided by the aforementioned distributions yum and apt-get.

Follow these steps before upgrading Elasticsearch:

1. Always look at breaking changes first at www.elastic.co/guide/en/elasticsearch/reference/current/breaking-changes.html.

2. It is recommended that you test upgrades on development servers. Upgrading Elasticsearch on a production environment can creak things.

3. The most important rule is to always take backups before any upgrades on a production server.

To upgrade follow these steps:

1. Shut down Elasticsearch.

2. Upgrade it using a distributions package-management system, such as yum or apt-get.

3. Upgrade plug-ins, if any.

4. Start Elasticsearch.

You can upgrade plug-ins by changing the directory to /usr/share/elasticsearch. Once inside the directory, first list the plug-ins that are installed.

```
[vishne0@localhost elasticsearch]$ sudo bin/plugin list
```

First, you must remove the plug-in you want to upgrade.

```
[vishne0@localhost elasticsearch]$ sudo bin/plugin remove pluginname
```

To install a plug-in, do the following:

```
[vishne0@localhost elasticsearch]$ sudo bin/plugin install pluginname
```

Summary

In this chapter, you were introduced to Elasticsearch, including

- Installing Elasticsearch on CentOS 7 and Ubuntu 16.04.1

- Configuring Elasticsearch

- Running and testing Elasticsearch

In the next chapter, you will learn how to install Kibana, the graphical interface designed to work with Elasticsearch.

CHAPTER 3

■ ■ ■

Getting Started with Kibana

In earlier chapters, we installed Logstash and Elasticsearch successfully. Searching logs manually in Logstash can be a bit of a tedious process for beginners. We need something with which we can search our logs easily and quickly. And now we have a tool that works with Elasticsearch to allow us to do just that—Kibana.

Kibana is an open source web interface tool for Elasticsearch. We can access it with your browser. Kibana is an excellent tool for visualizing data in the form of charts, graphs, maps, and tables. So, when all we need is something that is pleasing to the eye and simple to understand as well, Kibana is the perfect choice.

We can search logs to check screens for, say, high loads on some of our nodes, or perhaps failed login attempts on SSH. Kibana provides various screens on which we can search, filter, and submit queries as well as view visual aspects, such as traffic peaks on a web site at a given time of day.

Installing Kibana is very simple. It doesn't require any coding or too many changes to configuration files to make it work.

Now let's move on and install Kibana on CentOS 7 and Ubuntu 16.04.1 LTS machines. For now, we do not require anything other than Elasticsearch, which we have already installed.

Installing Kibana on CentOS 7

Let's now install Kibana on CentOS 7, using yum. First, we will create a repo for Kibana, as shown in Figure 3-1.

```
[vishne0@centylog /]$ sudo vi /etc/yum.repos.d/kibana.repo
```

```
[vishne0@centylog /]$ sudo vi /etc/yum.repos.d/kibana.repo
```

Figure 3-1. Creating a repository in CentOS 7

Next, we will write the following code in our new repo to get the package, using yum (see Figure 3-2).

```
[kibana]
name=Kibana Repo
baseurl=http://packages.elastic.co/kibana/4.6/centos
gpgcheck=1
gpgkey=http://packages.elastic.co/GPG-KEY-elasticsearch
enabled=1
```

```
[kibana]
name=Kibana repository
baseurl=http://packages.elastic.co/kibana/4.6/centos
gpgcheck=1
gpgkey=http://packages.elastic.co/GPG-KEY-elasticsearch
enabled=1
```

Figure 3-2. *Writing code for our new Kibana repository*

As we have now created our repo, we will install Kibana using yum. Type the following command into your terminal window and press Enter (see Figure 3-3).

```
[vishne0@centylog /]$ sudo yum install kibana
```

```
[vishne0@centylog /]$ sudo yum install kibana
```

Figure 3-3. *Installing Kibana*

Once you press Enter, yum will install Kibana (see Figure 3-4).

```
[vishne0@centylog /]$ sudo yum install kibana
Loaded plugins: fastestmirror
base                                                                                    | 3.6 kB  00:00:00
elasticsearch-2.x                                                                       | 2.9 kB  00:00:00
epel/x86_64/metalink                                                                    | 5.0 kB  00:00:00
epel                                                                                    | 4.3 kB  00:00:00
extras                                                                                  | 3.4 kB  00:00:00
kibana                                                                                  | 2.9 kB  00:00:00
logstash-2.3                                                                            |  951 B  00:00:00
mysql-connectors-community                                                              | 2.5 kB  00:00:00
mysql-tools-community                                                                   | 2.5 kB  00:00:00
mysql56-community                                                                       | 2.5 kB  00:00:00
updates                                                                                 | 3.4 kB  00:00:00
(1/7): epel/x86_64/updateinfo                                                           |  632 kB  00:00:00
(2/7): epel/x86_64/primary_db                                                           | 4.2 MB  00:00:00
(3/7): extras/7/x86_64/primary_db                                                       |  165 kB  00:00:00
(4/7): mysql56-community/x86_64/primary_db                                              |  146 kB  00:00:00
(5/7): updates/7/x86_64/primary_db                                                      | 7.0 MB  00:00:00
(6/7): elasticsearch-2.x/primary_db                                                     | 7.3 kB  00:00:01
(7/7): kibana/primary_db                                                                |  17 kB  00:00:00
Determining fastest mirrors
 * base: mirrors.linode.com
 * epel: epel.mirror.angkasa.id
 * extras: mirrors.linode.com
 * updates: mirrors.linode.com
Resolving Dependencies
--> Running transaction check


--> Finished Dependency Resolution

Dependencies Resolved

=====================================================================================================================
 Package              Arch              Version              Repository              Size
=====================================================================================================================
Installing :
 kibana               x86_64            4.6.1-1              kibana                  33 M

Transaction Summary
=====================================================================================================================
```

Figure 3-4. *Kibana installed, using* yum *on CentOS 7*

As you see in Figure 3-4, Kibana is now installed on our CentOS 7 machine, and we will add the following code, so that it starts automatically on booting up.

On the CentOS 7 terminal window, type the following command and press Enter.

```
[vishne0@centylog]$ sudo chkconfig --add kibana
```

Kibana is now added to our init system. Now let's check our installation, to make sure that we start Kibana (see Figure 3-5).

```
[vishne0@centylog /]$ sudo service kibana start
[sudo] password for vishne0:
kibana started
```

```
[vishne0@centylog /]$ sudo service kibana start
[sudo] password for vishne0:
kibana started
```

***Figure 3-5.** Starting Kibana*

Kibana is now running. By default, it listens on localhost only on port 5601. To access the dashboard on port 5601, add the port to the firewall.

```
[vishne0@centylog /]$ firewall-cmd --zone=dmz --add-port=5601/tcp
```

We have opened port 5601. Start the web browser and open the following URL:

```
http://localhost:5601
```

In my case, I have set it up so that I will access it using my public IP (see Figure 3-6).

```
http://myip:5601
```

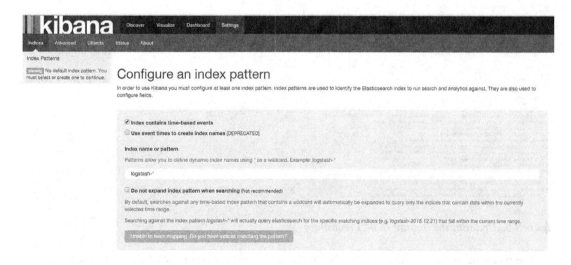

***Figure 3-6.** Accessing the Kibana interface*

Hurray! Our installation is successful, and Kibana is running. We will configure it and make it work in a subsequent section of this chapter.

Installing Kibana on Ubuntu 16.04.1 LTS

Let's now install Kibana on Ubuntu 16.04.1. We will add the repository for Kibana to our Ubuntu system, as follows (see also Figure 3-7):

```
vishne0@Ubuntu:~$ echo "deb http://packages.elastic.co/kibana/4.6/debian stable main" | sudo
tee -a /etc/apt/sources.list.d/kibana.list
```

```
vishne0@Ubuntu:~$ echo "deb http://packages.elastic.co/kibana/4.6/debian stable main" | sudo tee -a /etc/apt/sources.list.d/kibana.list
[sudo] password for vishne0:
deb http://packages.elastic.co/kibana/4.6/debian stable main
```

Figure 3-7. *Creating a repository for Kibana in Ubuntu 16.04.1*

As we have now added the Kibana repo, we will install it using apt-get on Ubuntu. First, we will update the repository with the following command (see Figure 3-8):

```
vishne0@Ubuntu:~$ sudo apt-get update
```

```
Hit http://packages.elasticsearch.org stable/main i386 Packages
Get:4 http://packages.elastic.co stable Release [1,234 B]
Get:5 http://security.ubuntu.com trusty-security/universe Sources [33.3 kB]
Hit http://packages.elastic.co stable/main amd64 Packages
Get:6 http://security.ubuntu.com trusty-security/main amd64 Packages [430 kB]
Hit http://packages.elastic.co stable/main i386 Packages
Get:7 http://security.ubuntu.com trusty-security/universe amd64 Packages [124 kB]
Ign http://mirrors.digitalocean.com trusty InRelease
Get:8 http://security.ubuntu.com trusty-security/main i386 Packages [403 kB]
Get:9 http://packages.elastic.co stable/main amd64 Packages [492 B]
Get:10 http://mirrors.digitalocean.com trusty-updates InRelease [65.9 kB]
Get:11 http://security.ubuntu.com trusty-security/universe i386 Packages [124 kB]
Get:12 http://packages.elastic.co stable/main i386 Packages [354 B]
Get:13 http://security.ubuntu.com trusty-security/main Translation-en [235 kB]
Get:14 http://security.ubuntu.com trusty-security/universe Translation-en [72.9 kB]
Ign http://packages.elasticsearch.org stable/main Translation-en_US
Hit http://mirrors.digitalocean.com trusty Release.gpg
Ign http://packages.elasticsearch.org stable/main Translation-en
Get:15 http://mirrors.digitalocean.com trusty-updates/main Sources [261 kB]
Get:16 http://mirrors.digitalocean.com trusty-updates/universe Sources [150 kB]
Ign http://packages.elastic.co stable/main Translation-en_US
Ign http://packages.elastic.co stable/main Translation-en
Ign http://packages.elastic.co stable/main Translation-en_US
Get:17 http://mirrors.digitalocean.com trusty-updates/main amd64 Packages [712 kB]
Ign http://packages.elastic.co stable/main Translation-en
Get:18 http://mirrors.digitalocean.com trusty-updates/universe amd64 Packages [338 kB]
Get:19 http://mirrors.digitalocean.com trusty-updates/main i386 Packages [691 kB]
Get:20 http://mirrors.digitalocean.com trusty-updates/universe i386 Packages [339 kB]
Hit http://mirrors.digitalocean.com trusty-updates/main Translation-en
Hit http://mirrors.digitalocean.com trusty-updates/universe Translation-en
Hit http://mirrors.digitalocean.com trusty Release
Hit http://mirrors.digitalocean.com trusty/main Sources
Hit http://mirrors.digitalocean.com trusty/universe Sources
Hit http://mirrors.digitalocean.com trusty/main amd64 Packages
Hit http://mirrors.digitalocean.com trusty/universe amd64 Packages
Hit http://mirrors.digitalocean.com trusty/main i386 Packages
Hit http://mirrors.digitalocean.com trusty/universe i386 Packages
Hit http://mirrors.digitalocean.com trusty/main Translation-en
Hit http://mirrors.digitalocean.com trusty/universe Translation-en
Ign http://mirrors.digitalocean.com trusty/main Translation-en_US
Ign http://mirrors.digitalocean.com trusty/universe Translation-en_US
Fetched 4,156 kB in 21s (195 kB/s)
```

Figure 3-8. *Updating the Ubuntu 16.04.1 repository*

Our repository is updated, and now it's the time to install Kibana on our Ubuntu machine, using the following command (see Figure 3-9):

```
vishne0@Ubuntu:~$ sudo apt-get install kibana
```

```
vishne0@Ubuntu:~$ sudo apt-get install kibana
Reading package lists... Done
Building dependency tree
Reading state information... Done
The following packages will be installed:
  kibana
0 upgraded, 1 newly installed, 0 to remove and 25 not upgraded.
Need to get 34.4 MB of archives.
After this operation, 1,703 kB of additional disk space will be used.
Get:1 https://packages.elastic.co/kibana/4.6/debian/ stable/main kibana amd64 4.6.1 [34.4 MB]
Fetched 34.4 MB in 17s (1,954 kB/s)
(Reading database ... 135698 files and directories currently installed.)
Preparing to unpack .../kibana_4.6.1_amd64.deb ...
Stopping kibana service... OK
Unpacking kibana (4.6.1)
Processing triggers for ureadahead (0.100.0-16) ...
Setting up kibana (4.6.1) ...

Processing triggers for ureadahead (0.100.0-16)
```

Figure 3-9. Installing Kibana on Ubuntu 16.04.1

Now that Kibana is installed on your machine, you have to add the following command, so that it starts automatically on booting up (see Figure 3-10):

vishne0@Ubuntu:~$ sudo update-rc.d kibana defaults 95 10

```
vishne0@Ubuntu:~$ sudo update-rc.d kibana defaults 95 10

Adding system startup for /etc/init.d/kibana ...
   /etc/rc0.d/K10kibana -> ../init.d/kibana
   /etc/rc1.d/K10kibana -> ../init.d/kibana
   /etc/rc6.d/K10kibana -> ../init.d/kibana
   /etc/rc2.d/S95kibana -> ../init.d/kibana
   /etc/rc3.d/S95kibana -> ../init.d/kibana
   /etc/rc4.d/S95kibana -> ../init.d/kibana
   /etc/rc5.d/S95kibana -> ../init.d/kibana
```

Figure 3-10. Adding Kibana to boot

OK. It's time to test our installation, as we did previously for our CentOS 7 machine. Again, by default, Kibana is accessible from localhost on port 5601 by typing the following command into your web browser:

http://localhost:5601

In my case, I will access it using my public IP (see Figure 3-11).

http://myip:5601

```
vishne0@Ubuntu:~$ sudo service kibana start
```

Figure 3-11. *Starting Kibana on Ubuntu 16.04.1*

Before accessing it from your browser, you have to start it on your system, so type the following command into your terminal (see Figure 3-11):

```
vishne0@Ubuntu:~$ sudo service kibana start
```

It has started and is now running on default port 5601. Open your browser and type `http://localhost:5601` or, on your IP, `http://myip:5601`.

On my Ubuntu system, I see the screen shown in Figure 3-12, as we saw earlier on the CentOS 7 system.

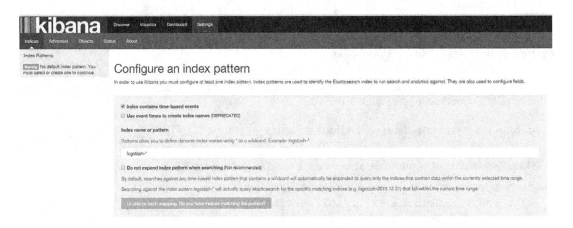

Figure 3-12. *Accessing the Kibana interface on Ubuntu 16.04.1*

One important thing to note here is that we have opened port 5601 on our firewall. If we are on a public IP, this will result in a security issue. Kibana itself doesn't come with an authentication method. To secure Kibana, you have to use a reverse proxy such as Nginx or skip to Chapter 8 to read more about how to secure the ELK Stack.

Configuring Kibana with Logstash and Elasticsearch

Now that Kibana is installed, let's move forward to see what screens it provides. Let's also configure it with Elasticsearch, to see some demo data.

I have Apache installed on my server, and I will get some sample data from the Apache log to show you how Kibana works. Make sure that Logstash, Elasticsearch, and Kibana are all running.

First, I will create a sample configuration file for Apache logs with the following command (see Figure 3-13):

```
[vishne0@centylog /]$ sudo vi /etc/logstash/conf.d/01-webserver.conf
```

```
[vishne0@centylog /]$ sudo vi /etc/logstash/conf.d/01-webserver.conf
```

Figure 3-13. *Creating a sample configuration file for Kibana*

I will then include the following code in our configuration file (see Figure 3-14). (I will not explain the configuration file here, as you will learn about it in the next chapter.)

```
input {
  file {
    path => "/var/httpd/logs/access_log"
    start_position => "beginning"
  }
}
filter {
if [type] == "apache-access"
{
    grok {
      match => { "message" => "%{COMBINEDAPACHELOG}" }
    }
  }
  date {
    match => [ "timestamp" , "dd/MMM/yyyy:HH:mm:ss Z" ]
  }
}
output {
  elasticsearch {
    hosts => ["localhost:9200"]
  }
  stdout { codec => rubydebug }
}
```

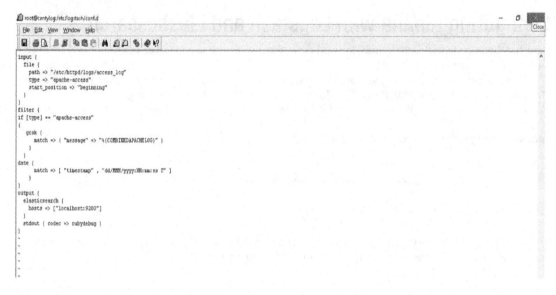

Figure 3-14. *Logstash configuration file for Apache access log*

Now I will run Logstash to generate the index (see Figure 3-15).

```
[vishne0@centylog /]$sudo service logstash  start
```

```
[vishne0@centylog /]$ sudo service logstash restart
```

Figure 3-15. *Restarting Logstash to generate the index*

Now I open another terminal screen, and issue the following command (see Figure 3-16).

```
[vishne0@centylog /]$  curl -XGET http://localhost:9200/_cat/indices?v
health status  index               pri rep docs.count docs.deleted store.size pri.store.size
yellow open    logstash-2016.03.08  5   1      139          0        157.2kb       157.2kb
yellow open    logstash-2016.03.07  5   1      4059         0         1.9mb         1.9mb
yellow open    .kibana              1   1       1           0         3.1kb         3.1kb
```

```
[vishne0@centylog /]$  curl -XGET http://localhost:9200/_cat/indices?v
health status index                  pri rep docs.count docs.deleted
store.size pri.store.size
yellow open    logstash-2016.03.08  5   1         139          0
157.2kb        157.2kb
yellow open    logstash-2016.03.07  5   1         4059         0
1.9mb          1.9mb
yellow open    .kibana              1   1          1           0
3.1kb          3.1kb
```

Figure 3-16.

You will see the preceding output shown in Figure 3-16. You can see the two indexes that I created with Logstash. You will see that the Logstash indexes are in the format of YYY-MM-DD. After the indexes are created, go to your browser with Kibana open and type logstash-* to match your index pattern. Keep it that way, and press Enter once it's done. In the other dialog box, you will see the Time-field name, where it will show @timestamp (see Figure 3-17).

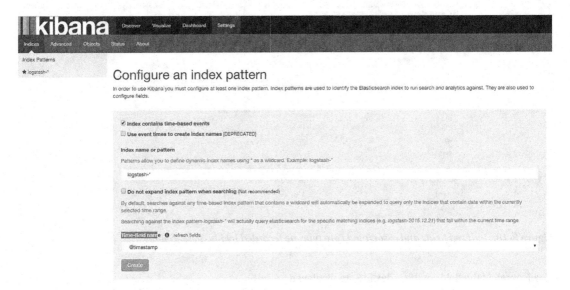

Figure 3-17. *Creating an index pattern on the Kibana interface*

Now click Create, and the screen shown in Figure 3-18 will appear.

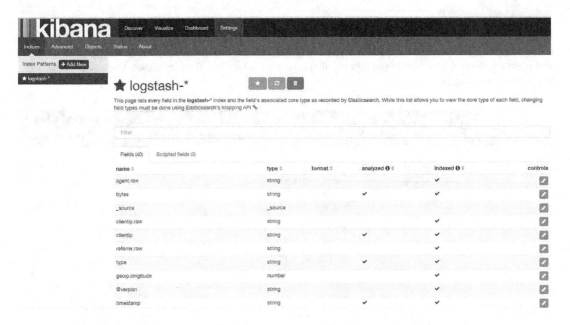

Figure 3-18. *Indexed fields and associated core type, as recorded by Elasticsearch*

Now all of the fields of the index file are displayed.

Next, let's see what Kibana screens are available. If you click Discover at the top left, you will see a screen similar to the one shown in Figure 3-19.

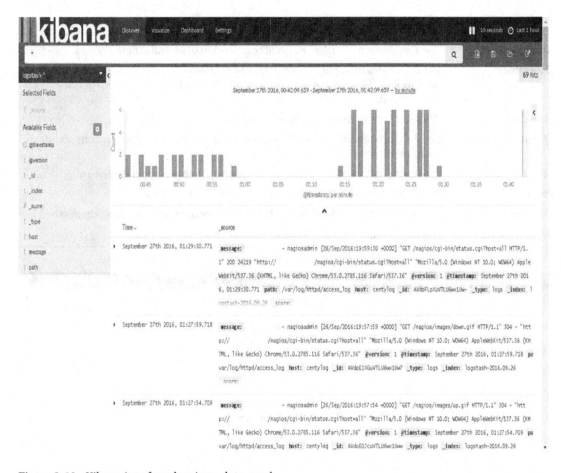

Figure 3-19. *Kibana interface showing a data graph*

You see the histograms here and the data from the access_log, as configured in 01-webserver.conf.

You can submit your search here and see the results. For example, you are looking at the data of the Apache access_log, so you can search for the code 200. In the Search box, type 200 and press Enter, and you will see the result.

At right side of the Search box, you have a few options, such as New search, Save search, Load a saved search, and Share a search.

Kibana Visualize

Once you are logged into the Kibana dashboard, just after the Discover tab, there is a tab for Visualize. Kibana supports different types of visualization methods (see Table 3-1), which you can use for your data. Click the Visualize tab, and a screen similar to the one shown in Figure 3-20 will open.

Table 3-1. *Kibana Visualization Types*

Area chart	Use area charts to visualize the total contribution of several different series.
Data table	Use data tables to display the raw data of a composed aggregation. You can display the data table for several other visualizations by clicking at the bottom of the visualization.
Line chart	Use line charts to compare different series.
Markdown widget	Use the markdown widget to display free-form information or instructions about your dashboard.
Metric	Use the metric visualization to display a single number on your dashboard.
Pie chart	Use pie charts to display each source's contribution to a total.
Tile map	Use tile maps to associate the results of an aggregation with geographic points.
Vertical bar chart	Use vertical bar charts as a general-purpose chart.

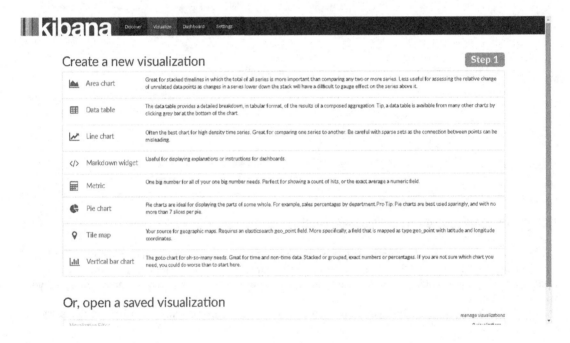

Figure 3-20. *Kibana Visualize*

You can also enable auto-refresh for the page with the latest data. To enable auto-refresh, click the clock icon at the top right, and you will see a screen with time intervals similar to those seen in Figure 3-21.

Figure 3-21. *Options for timed intervals*

Here, at the top right, you can see the auto-refresh option. If you click that, you will see the auto-refresh timed intervals. I have selected the option of 10 seconds (Figure 3-22). So now, my page will auto-refresh every 10 seconds, with a new set of data coming from the indexes I have created.

Figure 3-22. *Timed intervals for auto-refresh option*

Kibana Plug-ins

Kibana has a lot of plug-ins for additional functionality. To see the list of the installed plug-ins, change the directory to /opt/kibana.

```
[vishne0@centylog /]$ cd /opt/kibana/
```

Once you are inside the directory, issue the following command:

```
[vishne0@centylog kibana]$ sudo bin/kibana plugin –list
```

In this case, no plug-ins were installed, so there is no list. To add plug-ins, simply run the following command:

```
[vishne0@centylog kibana]$ [vishne0@centylog kibana]$ bin/kibana plugin -i
<org>/<package>/<version>
```

Here, org refers to *organization*, so if you want to install all the plug-ins from Elasticsearch, you install these with the following command (see Figure 3-23):

```
[vishne0@centylog kibana]$ sudo  bin/kibana plugin -i elasticsearch/graph/latest
```

41

```
[vishne0@centylog kibana]$ sudo  bin/kibana plugin -i elasticsearch/graph/latest
[sudo] password for vishne0:
Installing graph
Attempting to transfer from https://download.elastic.co/elasticsearch/graph/graph-latest.tar.gz
Transferring 69171 bytes...................
Transfer complete
Extracting plugin archive
Extraction complete
Optimizing and caching browser bundles...
Plugin installation complete
[vishne0@centylog kibana]$ █
```

Figure 3-23. *Installing plug-ins for Kibana*

As shown in Figure 3-23, the plug-in Graphs from Elasticsearch is installed. We can install the plug-in from a URL as well:

```
[vishne0@centylog kibana]$ sudo  bin/kibana plugin -i  pluginname  -u  url
```

We can check a list of all available plug-ins at: https://github.com/elastic/kibana/wiki/Known-Plugins.

Removing Plug-ins

We can remove a plug-in by running the following command:

```
[vishne0@centylog kibana]$ sudo  bin/kibana plugin --remove graph
Removing graph...
```

It's so simple isn't it?

Updating a Plug-in

To update a plug-in in Kibana, we have to remove the existing version of plug-in first and then install the latest one.

Kibana Server Configuration

The Kibana server reads its server properties from the kibana.yml configuration file. By default, Kibana runs on port 5601, so you do not have to make many changes to the configuration file. The configuration file contents are shown in Table 3-2.

Table 3-2. *Kibana Configuration Properties*

`server.port:`	Default: 5601 Kibana is served by a back-end server. This setting specifies the port to use.
`server.host:`	Default: `"0.0.0.0"`. This setting specifies the IP address of the back-end server.
`server.basePath:`	Use to specify a path to mount Kibana, if you are running behind a proxy. This setting cannot end in a slash (`/`).
`server.maxPayloadBytes:`	Default: 1048576. The maximum payload size in bytes for incoming server requests.
`elasticsearch.url:`	Default: `http://localhost:9200`. The URL of the Elasticsearch instance to use for all your queries.
`kibana.index:`	Default: `.kibana`. Kibana uses an index in Elasticsearch to store saved searches, visualizations, and dashboards. Kibana creates a new index, if the index doesn't already exist.
`kibana.defaultAppId:`	Default: `discover`. The default application to load.
`tilemap.url:`	Default:`https://tiles.elastic.co/v1/default/{z}/{x}/{y}.png?elastic_tile_service_tos=agree&my_app_name=kibana`. The URL to the tile service that Kibana uses to display map tiles in tilemap visualizations.
`tilemap.options.minZoom:`	Default: 1. The minimum zoom level.
`tilemap.options.maxZoom:`	Default: 10. The maximum zoom level.
`tilemap.options.attribution:`	Default: `© [Elastic Tile Service](https://www.elastic.co/elastic-tile-service)`. The map attribution string.
`tilemap.options.subdomains:`	An array of subdomains used by the tile service. Specifies the position of the subdomain in the URL with the token `{s}`.
`elasticsearch.username:` and `elasticsearch.password:`	If Elasticsearch is protected with basic authentication, these settings provide the username and password that the Kibana server uses to perform maintenance on the Kibana index at startup. Kibana users must still authenticate with Elasticsearch, which is proxied through the Kibana server.
`server.ssl.cert:` and `server.ssl.key:`	Paths to the PEM-format SSL certificate and SSL key files, respectively. These files enable SSL for outgoing requests from the Kibana server to the browser.
`elasticsearch.ssl.cert:` and `elasticsearch.ssl.key:`	Optional settings that provide the paths to the PEM-format SSL certificate and key files. These files validate that your Elasticsearch back end uses the same key files.
`elasticsearch.ssl.ca:`	Optional setting that enables you to specify a path to the PEM file for the certificate authority for your Elasticsearch instance
`elasticsearch.ssl.verify:`	Default: `true`.To disregard the validity of SSL certificates, change this setting's value to `false`.
`elasticsearch.pingTimeout:`	Default: The value of the `elasticsearch.requestTimeout` setting. Time in milliseconds to wait for Elasticsearch to respond to pings

(*continued*)

Table 3-2. (*continued*)

`elasticsearch.requestTimeout:`	Default: 30000. Time in milliseconds to wait for responses from the back end or Elasticsearch. This value must be a positive integer.
`elasticsearch.shardTimeout:`	Default: 0. Time in milliseconds for Elasticsearch to wait for responses from shards. Set this to 0 to disable.
`pid.file:`	This specifies the path where Kibana creates the process ID file.
`logging.dest:`	Default: `stdout`. This enables you specify a file where Kibana stores log output.
`logging.filter.<key>:`	Default: authorization `Replace <key>` with the string to filter. Set the value of this setting to remove to remove matching keys from all logged objects. Set the value of this setting sensor to replace each character in the key's value with an X character.
`logging.silent:`	Default: `false`. Set the value of this setting to `true` to suppress all logging output.
`logging.quiet:`	Default: `false`. Set the value of this setting to `true` to suppress all logging output other than error messages.
`logging.verbose`	Default: `false`. Set the value of this setting to `true` to log all events, including system usage information and all requests.
`status.allowAnonymous`	Default: `false`. If authentication is enabled, setting this to `true` allows unauthenticated users to access the Kibana server status API and status page.

Summary

In this chapter, you learned how to configure Kibana with Logstash and Elasticsearch. You also learned how to configure index patterns, as well as the following:

- The Kibana dashboard

- Kibana Visualize

- How to add, remove, and update Kibana plug-ins

- Kibana configuration properties

In the next chapter, you will see how to configure remote servers, to send inputs to our ELK Stack server, using Filebeat.

CHAPTER 4

■ ■ ■

Working with Remote Servers

Setting Up Logstash on a Remote Server

In previous chapters, we installed Logstash, Elasticsearch, and Kibana. We configured an ELK Stack on a single server and also tested it. Running an ELK Stack on a single server, however, is not very useful. Our goal is to set up a centralized logging system for all of our servers, running at different locations and hosting web sites, web applications, ERP, and CRM systems. By setting up a centralized logging system, we can monitor the performance of our servers and analyze the logs for any issue that arises. Thus, in this chapter, you will see how we can ship events from remote servers to our ELK Stack server.

To ship events from a remote server, we will use the Filebeat shipper. Filebeat is a data shipper based on the Logstash forwarder. It is installed as an agent on servers from which we want to send data to our centralized log system. The best part of Filebeat is that it monitors the logs, takes the files, and ships them to Logstash for parsing, or we can send the Filebeat events to Elasticsearch directly for indexing.

Figure 4-1 illustrates how Filebeat works with the ELK Stack:

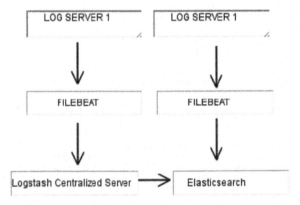

Figure 4-1. *Filebeat sends events to Logstash, or it can send them directly to Elasticsearch*

Installing Filebeat on a Remote CentOS 7 Server

Now let's start by installing Filebeat on our CentOS 7 server. First, we will download and install the public signing key.

```
vishne0@srv [~]# sudo rpm --import https://packages.elastic.co/GPG-KEY-elasticsearch
```

Now let's create the repo file in `/etc/yum.repos.d/` with the name `filebeat.repo`.

```
vishne0@srv [~]# sudo vi /etc/yum.repos.d/filebeat.repo
```

Press i to insert the code into the file.

```
[Filebeat]
name= Filebeat Repository
baseurl=https://packages.elastic.co/beats/yum/el/$basearch
enabled=1
gpgkey=https://packages.elastic.co/GPG-KEY-elasticsearch
gpgcheck=1
```

Press Esc and then `:wq` to exit the editor, as shown in Figure 4-2.

```
[Filebeat]
name=Filebeat Repository
baseurl=https://packages.elastic.co/beats/yum/el/$basearch
enabled=1
gpgkey=https://packages.elastic.co/GPG-KEY-elasticsearch
gpgcheck=1
~
~
```

Figure 4-2. *Creating Filebeat repo in CentOS 7 server*

Now that our repository is ready, let's install Filebeat (see Figure 4-3).

```
Resolving Dependencies
--> Running transaction check
---> Package filebeat.x86_64 0:1.3.1-1 will be installed
--> Finished Dependency Resolution

Dependencies Resolved

================================================================================================================
 Package                 Arch                  Version                  Repository                       Size
================================================================================================================
Installing:
 filebeat                x86_64                1.3.1-1                  Filebeat                        4.0 M

Transaction Summary
================================================================================================================
Install  1 Package

Total download size: 4.0 M
Installed size: 4.0 M
Is this ok [y/d/N]: y
Downloading packages:
warning: /var/cache/yum/x86_64/7/Filebeat/packages/filebeat-1.3.1-x86_64.rpm: Header V4 RSA/SHA1 Signature, key ID d88e42b4: NOKEY=============         ] 771 kB/s | 3.3 MB  00:00:00 ETA
Public key for filebeat-1.3.1-x86_64.rpm is not installed
filebeat-1.3.1-x86_64.rpm                                                                   | 4.0 MB  00:00:18
Retrieving key from https://packages.elastic.co/GPG-KEY-elasticsearch
Importing GPG key 0xD88E42B4:
 Userid     : "Elasticsearch (Elasticsearch Signing Key) <dev_ops@elasticsearch.org>"
 Fingerprint: 4609 5acc 8548 582c 1a26 99a9 d27d 666c d88e 42b4
 From       : https://packages.elastic.co/GPG-KEY-elasticsearch
Is this ok [y/N]: y
Running transaction check
Running transaction test
Transaction test succeeded
Running transaction
  Installing : filebeat-1.3.1-1.x86_64                                                                      1/1
  Verifying  : filebeat-1.3.1-1.x86_64                                                                      1/1

Installed:
  filebeat.x86_64 0:1.3.1-1

Complete!
```

Figure 4-3. *Installing Filebeat on a CentOS 7 server, using yum*

Filebeat is now installed, so let's configure it to run at boot up.

```
vishne0@srv [~]# sudo chkconfig --add filebeat
```

Now it's added to boot up as well.
Next, let's Install Filebeat on Ubuntu16.04.1 LTS.

Installing Filebeat on a Remote Ubuntu 16.04.1 LTS Server

To install Filebeat on our remote Ubuntu server, we will first download and install the public signing key, as follows:

```
vishne0@bckeventaa:/root$ curl https://packages.elasticsearch.org/GPG-KEY-elasticsearch |
sudo apt-key add -
```

Next, we will add a repository file to /etc/apt/sources.list.d/filebeat.list.

```
vishne0@bckeventaa:/$ echo "deb https://packages.elastic.co/beats/apt stable main" | sudo
tee -a /etc/apt/sources.list.d/filebeat.list
```

We have now created the repository file. Next, let's update our system by running the following command (see Figure 4-4):

```
vishne0@bckeventaa:/$ sudo apt-get update
```

```
vishne0@snf-725573:~$ sudo apt-get update
Hit:1 http://ftp.cc.uoc.gr/mirrors/linux/ubuntu/packages xenial InRelease
Get:2 http://ftp.cc.uoc.gr/mirrors/linux/ubuntu/packages xenial-updates InRelease [95.7 kB]
Hit:3 http://ftp.cc.uoc.gr/mirrors/linux/ubuntu/packages xenial-backports InRelease
Hit:4 http://security.ubuntu.com/ubuntu xenial-security InRelease
Ign:5 https://packages.elastic.co/beats/apt stable InRelease
Get:6 https://packages.elastic.co/beats/apt stable Release [1,797 B]
Get:7 https://packages.elastic.co/beats/apt stable Release.gpg [473 B]
Get:8 https://packages.elastic.co/beats/apt stable/main amd64 Packages [5,896 B]
Get:9 https://packages.elastic.co/beats/apt stable/main i386 Packages [5,808 B]
Fetched 110 kB in 2s (43.8 kB/s)
Reading package lists... Done
```

Figure 4-4. *Running the apt-get update*

Our repository is updated, so now let's install Filebeat (see Figure 4-5).

```
vishne0@bckeventaa:/$ sudo apt-get install filebeat
```

```
vishne0@snf-725573:~$ sudo apt-get install filebeat
Reading package lists... Done
Building dependency tree
Reading state information... Done
The following NEW packages will be installed:
  filebeat
0 upgraded, 1 newly installed, 0 to remove and 3 not upgraded.
Need to get 4,255 kB of archives.
After this operation, 12.6 MB of additional disk space will be used.
Get:1 https://packages.elastic.co/beats/apt stable/main amd64 filebeat amd64 1.3.1 [4,255 kB]
Fetched 4,255 kB in 5s (716 kB/s)
Selecting previously unselected package filebeat.
(Reading database ... 59720 files and directories currently installed.)
Preparing to unpack .../filebeat_1.3.1_amd64.deb ...
Unpacking filebeat (1.3.1) ...
Processing triggers for systemd (229-4ubuntu11) ...
Processing triggers for ureadahead (0.100.0-19) ...
Setting up filebeat (1.3.1) ...
Processing triggers for systemd (229-4ubuntu11) ...
Processing triggers for ureadahead (0.100.0-19) ...
vishne0@snf-725573:~$
```

Figure 4-5. *Installing Filebeat on a remote Ubuntu server*

We now add Filebeat to /etc/init.d, so that it starts automatically during boot up (see Figure 4-6).

vishne0@bckeventaa:/$ sudo update-rc.d filebeat defaults 95 10

```
vishne0@snf-725573:~$ sudo update-rc.d filebeat defaults 95 10
vishne0@snf-725573:~$ ▮
```

Figure 4-6. *Adding Filebeat to start automatically at boot up*

Configuring Filebeat on CentOS 7 and Ubuntu 16.04.1 LTS

We are now ready to configure Filebeat for both CentOS 7 and Ubuntu 16.04.1 LTS. The configuration file is placed at /etc/filebeat/filebeat.yml.

Let's configure Filebeat on CentOS 7 first. Open the /etc/filebeat/filebeat.yml file (see Figure 4-7).

vishne0@srv [/home]# sudo vi /etc/filebeat/filebeat.yml

```
▌################## Filebeat Configuration Example ########################

############################# Filebeat ####################################
filebeat:
  # List of prospectors to fetch data.
  prospectors:
    # Each - is a prospector. Below are the prospector specific configurations
    -

      # Paths that should be crawled and fetched. Glob based paths.
      # To fetch all ".log" files from a specific level of subdirectories
      # /var/log/*/*.log can be used.
      # For each file found under this path, a harvester is started.
      # Make sure not file is defined twice as this can lead to unexpected behaviour.
      paths:
        - /var/log/*.log
        #- c:\programdata\elasticsearch\logs\*

      # Configure the file encoding for reading files with international characters
      # following the W3C recommendation for HTML5 (http://www.w3.org/TR/encoding).
      # Some sample encodings:
      #   plain, utf-8, utf-16be-bom, utf-16be, utf-16le, big5, gb18030, gbk,
      #    hz-gb-2312, euc-kr, euc-jp, iso-2022-jp, shift-jis, ...
      #encoding: plain

      # Type of the files. Based on this the way the file is read is decided.
      # The different types cannot be mixed in one prospector
      #
      # Possible options are:
      # * log: Reads every line of the log file (default)
      # * stdin: Reads the standard in
      input_type: log

      # Exclude lines. A list of regular expressions to match. It drops the lines that are
      # matching any regular expression from the list. The include_lines is called before
      # exclude_lines. By default, no lines are dropped.
      # exclude_lines: ["^DBG"]

      # Include lines. A list of regular expressions to match. It exports the lines that are
      # matching any regular expression from the list. The include_lines is called before
      # exclude_lines. By default, all the lines are exported.
      # include_lines: ["^ERR", "^WARN"]

      # Exclude files. A list of regular expressions to match. Filebeat drops the files that
"/etc/filebeat/filebeat.yml" 421L, 17104C
```

Figure 4-7. *Editing the* `filebeat.yml` *file*

Let me explain the configuration parameters just a bit, as shown in the following code snippet:

```
filebeat:
  # List of prospectors to fetch data.
  prospectors:
    # Each - is a prospector. Below are the prospector specific configurations
    -

      # Paths that should be crawled and fetched. Glob based paths.
      # To fetch all ".log" files from a specific level of subdirectories
      # /var/log/*/*.log can be used.
      # For each file found under this path, a harvester is started.
```

```
# Make sure not file is defined twice as this can lead to unexpected behaviour.
paths:
  - /var/log/*.log
  #- c:\programdata\elasticsearch\logs\*
```

Here, the line -/var/log/*.log, '-' is a prospector for a single path, which means that Filebeat will harvest all of the files with an extension .log within this path.

Now let's send the output to our centralized log server. We can send our output to Logstash or to Elasticsearch directly. Next, we will see how we can send the output to both Logstash and Elasticsearch.

Sending Output to Logstash Using Filebeat

First, go to the Logstash as output section in our filebeat.yml configuration file (see Figure 4-8).

```
### Logstash as output
#logstash:
  # The Logstash hosts
  #hosts: ["localhost:5044"]

  # Number of workers per Logstash host.
  #worker: 1

  # Set gzip compression level.
  #compression_level: 3

  # Optional load balance the events between the Logstash hosts
  #loadbalance: true

  # Optional index name. The default index name depends on the each beat.
  # For Packetbeat, the default is set to packetbeat, for Topbeat
  # top topbeat and for Filebeat to filebeat.
  #index: filebeat

  # Optional TLS. By default is off.
  #tls:
    # List of root certificates for HTTPS server verifications
    #certificate_authorities: ["/etc/pki/root/ca.pem"]

    # Certificate for TLS client authentication
    #certificate: "/etc/pki/client/cert.pem"

    # Client Certificate Key
    #certificate_key: "/etc/pki/client/cert.key"

    # Controls whether the client verifies server certificates and host name.
    # If insecure is set to true, all server host names and certificates will be
    # accepted. In this mode TLS based connections are susceptible to
    # man-in-the-middle attacks. Use only for testing.
    #insecure: true

    # Configure cipher suites to be used for TLS connections
    #cipher_suites: []

    # Configure curve types for ECDHE based cipher suites
    #curve_types: []
```

Figure 4-8. Logstash as output section in filebeat.yml

In the Logstash as output section, please uncomment the following line:

```
### Logstash as output
  logstash:
    # The Logstash hosts
    hosts: ["XXX.XXX.XX.XXX:5044"]
```

Here, I have removed # from the front of Logstash: and from hosts: and entered the IP address of the remote Logstash server we have set up. The port number, 5044, is written by default into the configuration file.

To receive inputs from Filebeat, we have to configure Logstash. So, let's go back to our centralized Logstash server and install the plug-in called logstash-input-beats (see Figure 4-9). Once logged in to the server, change the directory to /opt/logstash/bin. Inside bin, run the following command:

```
[vishne0@centylog bin]$ sudo ./plugin install logstash-input-beats
```

```
[vishne0@centylog bin]$ sudo ./plugin install logstash-input-beats
[sudo] password for vishne0:
Validating logstash-input-beats
Installing logstash-input-beats
Installation successful
[vishne0@centylog bin]$ _
```

Figure 4-9. *Installing the beats plug-in for Logstash to accept incoming beats connections*

Now that the plug-in is installed, let's configure Logstash to receive the connection at port 5044. Let's create a configuration file for Logstash to receive the input from Filebeat.

We will name the file 02-srv1.conf. Change the directory to /etc/logstash/conf.d.

```
[vishne0@centylog /]$ cd /etc/logstash/conf.d/
```

Now let's create the file:

```
[vishne0@centylog /]$ sudo vi /etc/logstash/conf.d/02-srv1.conf
```

Press I and put below code inside the file:

```
input {
  beats {
    port => 5044
  }
}

output {
  elasticsearch {
    hosts => "localhost:9200"
    index => "%{[@metadata][beat]}-%{+YYYY.MM.dd}"
    document_type => "%{[@metadata][type]}"
  }
}
```

If you examine the preceding input section, you will see the code regarding port 5044 and then the code that sends the output to Elasticsearch at port 9200.

Now restart Logstash on our centralized server. We also start Filebeat on our remote server.

To restart Logstash on our centralized server, issue the following command:

```
[vishne0@centylog /]$ sudo /etc/init.d/logstash restart
```

To start Filebeat on our remote server, issue the following command:

```
vishne0@srv [/etc/filebeat]# sudo /etc/init.d/filebeat start
```

Now it's time to check if we are receiving inputs, and Kibana comes handy here, as we already installed it in a previous chapter. Open your browser and type the following command:

```
http://yourip:5601
```

When I access Kibana, I see the screen shown in Figure 4-10.

Figure 4-10. *Filebeat input from the remote host to the centralized Logstash server on Kibana*

If you look at the output section in Figure 4-10, you will see that it displays beat.hostname, which comes from the remote server on which we have configured Filebeat. We have successfully sent the inputs using Filebeat to our Logstash server at our centralized logging server.

Now let's configure Filebeat to send the data to Elasticsearch directly.

Sending Data to Elasticsearch Using Filebeat

We have already seen how to send data from the remote server to our Logstash server. Sending data to Logstash works in such a way that Logstash receives the input and then forwards it to Elasticsearch, which indexes the data and sends the output to Kibana. Now we will configure Filebeat to send data to Elasticsearch only, which will remove Logstash from the chain of events.

To configure Filebeat, we first have to go to our remote server and comment out the Logstash configuration in `filebeat.yml` (also see Figure 4-11).

```
### Logstash as output
#  logstash:
    # The Logstash hosts
  #  hosts: ["1xx.1xx.1x.2xx:5044"]
```

```
  ### Logstash as output
#  logstash:
    # The Logstash hosts
  #  hosts: ["1xx.1xx.1x.xxx:5044"]

    # Number of workers per Logstash host.
    #worker: 1

    # Set gzip compression level.
    #compression_level: 3

    # Optional load balance the events between the Logstash hosts
    #loadbalance: true

    # Optional index name. The default index name depends on the each beat.
    # For Packetbeat, the default is set to packetbeat, for Topbeat
    # top topbeat and for Filebeat to filebeat.
    #index: filebeat

    # Optional TLS. By default is off.
    #tls:
      # List of root certificates for HTTPS server verifications
      #certificate_authorities: ["/etc/pki/root/ca.pem"]

      # Certificate for TLS client authentication
      #certificate: "/etc/pki/client/cert.pem"

      # Client Certificate Key
      #certificate_key: "/etc/pki/client/cert.key"

      # Controls whether the client verifies server certificates and host name.
      # If insecure is set to true, all server host names and certificates will be
      # accepted. In this mode TLS based connections are susceptible to
      # man-in-the-middle attacks. Use only for testing.
      #insecure: true

      # Configure cipher suites to be used for TLS connections
      #cipher_suites: []

      # Configure curve types for ECDHE based cipher suites
      #curve_types: []
```

Figure 4-11. *Disabling the Logstash section in* `filebeat.yml` *on remote host*

Now let's move forward and configure Filebeat to send beats to Elasticsearch. Open the Filebeat configuration file at /etc/filebeat/filebeat.yml.

```
vishne0@srv [/etc/filebeat]# sudo vi filebeat.yml

### Elasticsearch as output
  elasticsearch:
    # Array of hosts to connect to.
    # Scheme and port can be left out and will be set to the default (http and 9200)
# In case you specify and additional path, the scheme is required:  http://localhost:9200/
path
    # IPv6 addresses should always be defined as: https://[2001:db8::1]:9200
    hosts: ["youripaddress:9200"]
```

In the preceding code snippet in filebeat.yml, we have the field elasticsearch: and hosts:. In the hosts section, add the IP address of your remote server.

Now we have to load the index template for Elasticsearch, in order to know what fields it's going to analyze and how. Fortunately, the Filebeat package installs a template for us to use. So, we will now configure the filebeat.yml file to load the template, as shown in Figure 4-12.

```
#worker: 1

# Optional index name. The default is "filebeat" and generates
# [filebeat-]YYYY.MM.DD keys.
#index: "filebeat"

# A template is used to set the mapping in Elasticsearch
# By default template loading is disabled and no template is loaded.
# These settings can be adjusted to load your own template or overwrite existing ones
#template:

  # Template name. By default the template name is filebeat.
  name: "filebeat"

  # Path to template file
  path: "/etc/filebeat/filebeat.template.json"

  # Overwrite existing template
  #overwrite: false

# Optional HTTP Path
#path: "/elasticsearch"

# Proxy server url
#proxy_url: http://proxy:3128

# The number of times a particular Elasticsearch index operation is attempted. If
# the indexing operation doesn't succeed after this many retries, the events are
# dropped. The default is 3.
#max_retries: 3

# The maximum number of events to bulk in a single Elasticsearch bulk API index request.
# The default is 50.
#bulk_max_size: 50

# Configure http request timeout before failing an request to Elasticsearch.
#timeout: 90

# The number of seconds to wait for new events between two bulk API index requests.
# If `bulk_max_size` is reached before this interval expires, addition bulk index
# requests are made.
#flush_interval: 1
```

Figure 4-12. *Configuring* filebeat.yml *to load the Filebeat template*

The filebeat.template.json file resides in /etc/filebeat/. In our filebeat.yml file, we will include the path, so that Filebeat can load the template.

```
# A template is used to set the mapping in Elasticsearch
    # By default template loading is disabled and no template is loaded.
    # These settings can be adjusted to load your own template or overwrite existing ones
template:

    # Template name. By default the template name is filebeat.
    name: "filebeat"

    # Path to template file
    path: "filebeat.template.json"
```

We will keep the default name of the template as `filebeat`. Next, press Esc and then `:wq`, to save and exit from the `vi` editor. Let's restart Filebeat to apply changes with the following command:

```
vishne0@srv [/etc/filebeat]# sudo service filebeat restart
```

Next, we have to make some changes in the Elasticsearch configuration on our centralized logging server. In Chapter 2, we configured Elasticsearch to run on our localhost. However, for Filebeat to send inputs to Elasticsearch from a remote server, we have to run Elasticsearch on a public IP, as shown in Figure 4-13.

```
#
# --------------------------------- Network ---------------------------------
#
# Set the bind address to a specific IP (IPv4 or IPv6):
#
 network.host: localhost, ... ....... . 
 # network.host: 0.0.0.0
#
# Set a custom port for HTTP:
#
 http.port: 9200
#
# For more information, see the documentation at:
# <http://www.elastic.co/guide/en/elasticsearch/reference/current/modules-network.html>
#
# --------------------------------- Discovery ---------------------------------
#
# Pass an initial list of hosts to perform discovery when new node is started:
# The default list of hosts is ["127.0.0.1", "[::1]"]
#
# discovery.zen.ping.unicast.hosts: ["host1", "host2"]
#
# Prevent the "split brain" by configuring the majority of nodes (total number of nodes / 2 + 1):
#
# discovery.zen.minimum_master_nodes: 3
#
# For more information, see the documentation at:
# <http://www.elastic.co/guide/en/elasticsearch/reference/current/modules-discovery.html>
#
# --------------------------------- Gateway ---------------------------------
#
# Block initial recovery after a full cluster restart until N nodes are started:
#
# gateway.recover_after_nodes: 3
#
# For more information, see the documentation at:
# <http://www.elastic.co/guide/en/elasticsearch/reference/current/modules-gateway.html>
#
# --------------------------------- Various ---------------------------------
#
# Disable starting multiple nodes on a single system:
#
# node.max_local_storage_nodes: 1
```

Figure 4-13. *Configuring Elasticsearch to run on a public IP*

First, let's make a small change in our Elasticsearch configuration. Open `/etc/elasticsearch/elasticsearch.yml`.

```
[vishne0@centylog /]$ sudo vi /etc/elasticsearch/elasticsearch.yml
```

Next, we will go to the Network section of the configuration file.

We will now add our public IP to the network host, with the following command:

```
network.host: localhost, 0.0.0.0
```

Press Esc and then `:wq` to save the file. Once you have exited, restart Elasticsearch as follows:

```
[vishne0@centylog /]$ sudo /etc/init.d/elasticsearch restart
```

Next, let's check to see if Elasticsearch is running on our public IP (see Figure 4-14).

```
[vishne0@centylog elasticsearch]$  netstat -lntp | grep 9200
```

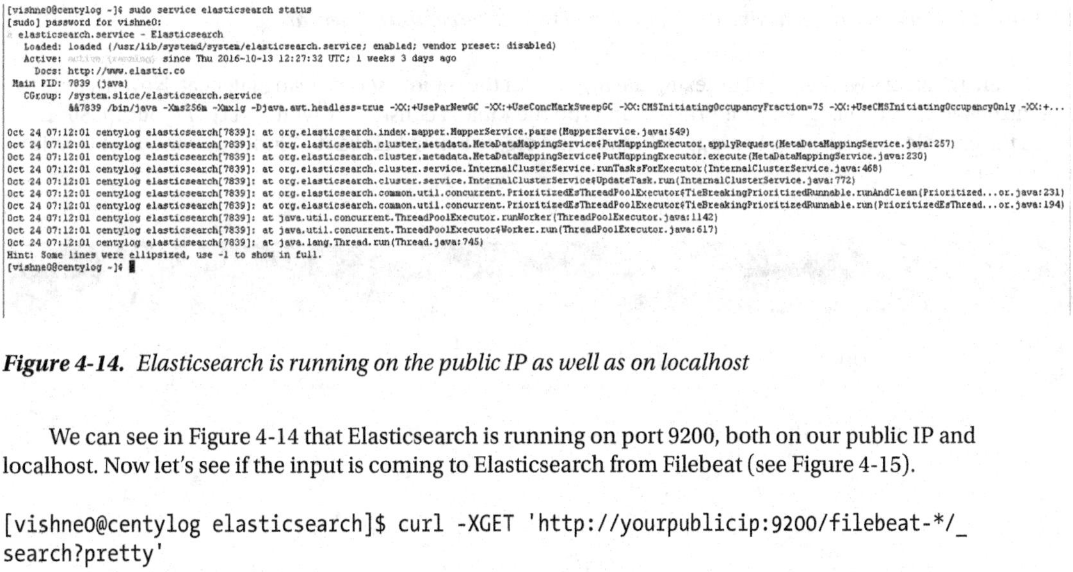

```
[vishne0@centylog ~]$ sudo service elasticsearch status
[sudo] password for vishne0:
  elasticsearch.service - Elasticsearch
   Loaded: loaded (/usr/lib/systemd/system/elasticsearch.service; enabled; vendor preset: disabled)
   Active: active (running) since Thu 2016-10-13 12:27:32 UTC; 1 weeks 3 days ago
     Docs: http://www.elastic.co
 Main PID: 7839 (java)
   CGroup: /system.slice/elasticsearch.service
           &&7839 /bin/java -Xms256m -Xmx1g -Djava.awt.headless=true -XX:+UseParNewGC -XX:+UseConcMarkSweepGC -XX:CMSInitiatingOccupancyFraction=75 -XX:+UseCMSInitiatingOccupancyOnly -XX:+...

Oct 24 07:12:01 centylog elasticsearch[7839]: at org.elasticsearch.index.mapper.MapperService.parse(MapperService.java:549)
Oct 24 07:12:01 centylog elasticsearch[7839]: at org.elasticsearch.cluster.metadata.MetaDataMappingService$PutMappingExecutor.applyRequest(MetaDataMappingService.java:257)
Oct 24 07:12:01 centylog elasticsearch[7839]: at org.elasticsearch.cluster.metadata.MetaDataMappingService$PutMappingExecutor.execute(MetaDataMappingService.java:230)
Oct 24 07:12:01 centylog elasticsearch[7839]: at org.elasticsearch.cluster.service.InternalClusterService.runTasksForExecutor(InternalClusterService.java:468)
Oct 24 07:12:01 centylog elasticsearch[7839]: at org.elasticsearch.cluster.service.InternalClusterService$UpdateTask.run(InternalClusterService.java:772)
Oct 24 07:12:01 centylog elasticsearch[7839]: at org.elasticsearch.common.util.concurrent.PrioritizedEsThreadPoolExecutor$TieBreakingPrioritizedRunnable.runAndClean(Prioritized...or.java:231)
Oct 24 07:12:01 centylog elasticsearch[7839]: at org.elasticsearch.common.util.concurrent.PrioritizedEsThreadPoolExecutor$TieBreakingPrioritizedRunnable.run(PrioritizedEsThread...or.java:194)
Oct 24 07:12:01 centylog elasticsearch[7839]: at java.util.concurrent.ThreadPoolExecutor.runWorker(ThreadPoolExecutor.java:1142)
Oct 24 07:12:01 centylog elasticsearch[7839]: at java.util.concurrent.ThreadPoolExecutor$Worker.run(ThreadPoolExecutor.java:617)
Oct 24 07:12:01 centylog elasticsearch[7839]: at java.lang.Thread.run(Thread.java:745)
Hint: Some lines were ellipsized, use -l to show in full.
[vishne0@centylog ~]$
```

Figure 4-14. *Elasticsearch is running on the public IP as well as on localhost*

We can see in Figure 4-14 that Elasticsearch is running on port 9200, both on our public IP and localhost. Now let's see if the input is coming to Elasticsearch from Filebeat (see Figure 4-15).

```
[vishne0@centylog elasticsearch]$ curl -XGET 'http://yourpublicip:9200/filebeat-*/_
search?pretty'
```

```
[vishne0@centylog ~]# curl -XGET 'http://localhost:9200/filebeat-*/_search?pretty'
{
  "took" : 348,
  "timed_out" : false,
  "_shards" : {
    "total" : 220,
    "successful" : 220,
    "failed" : 0
  },
  "hits" : {
    "total" : 8475552,
    "max_score" : 1.0,
    "hits" : [ {
      "_index" : "filebeat-2016.09.04",
      "_type" : "log",
      "_id" : "AVb1fxH3p7cQyTK921j9",
      "_score" : 1.0,
      "_source" : {
        "message" : "[2016-08-29 16:58:34 +0100] OOM check ....Done",
        "@version" : "1",
        "@timestamp" : "2016-09-04T13:59:07.141Z",
        "type" : "log",
        "count" : 1,
        "source" : "/var/log/chkservd.log",
        "offset" : 61327951,
        "input_type" : "log",
        "fields" : null,
        "beat" : {
          "hostname" : "srv.tux-hosting.com",
          "name" : "srv.tux-hosting.com"
        },
        "host" : "srv.tux-hosting.com",
        "tags" : [ "beats_input_codec_plain_applied" ]
      }
    }, {
      "_index" : "filebeat-2016.09.04",
      "_type" : "log",
      "_id" : "AVb1fxH3p7cQyTK921j-",
      "_score" : 1.0,
      "_source" : {
        "message" : "[2016-08-29 16:58:34 +0100] Service check ....spamd [[check command:+][socket connect:N/A]]...queueprocd [[check command:+][socket connect:N/A]]...p0f [[check command:+][
socket connect:N/A]]...nscd [[check command:N/A][socket connect:N/A]]...named [[check command:+][socket connect:N/A]]...mysql [[check command:+][socket connect:N/A]]...mailman [[check command
```

Figure 4-15. Elasticsearch indexing the input from a remote server using Filebeat

There we go. It's working and indexing the input from the remote server, using Filebeat. Now it's time to see the details in Kibana. Open your browser and run the Kibana console, by typing `http://yourip.5601`. Once the console is open, go to Settings ➤ Indices and create a new `filebeat-*` index pattern, as shown in Figure 4-16.

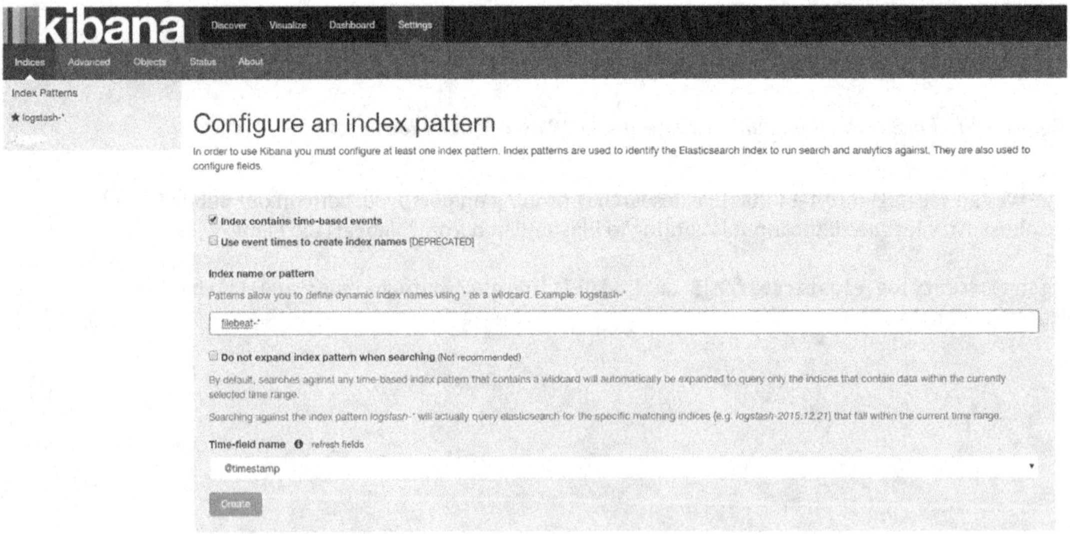

Figure 4-16. Creating new `filebeat-*` index pattern

Once we type filebeat-* and press Enter, it will display @timestamp in the Time-field name field. Now just click Create. After that, it will show all the fields of the filebeat-* index (see Figure 4-17).

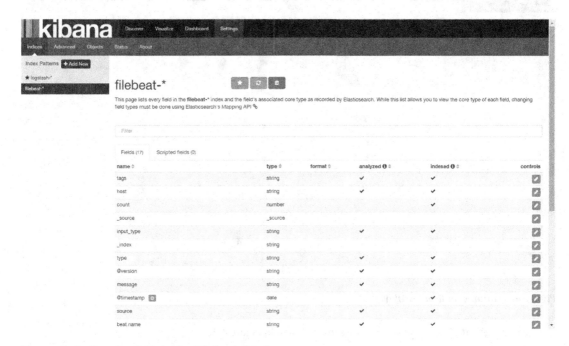

Figure 4-17. *Showing fields in the* filebeat-* *index*

Now click Discover at the top left. You will go to the dashboard where you can see below the search box the index pattern we have created in Chapter 2, with the name logstash-*. Click the drop-down icon next to it, and you will see our new filebeat-* index pattern (see Figure 4-18).

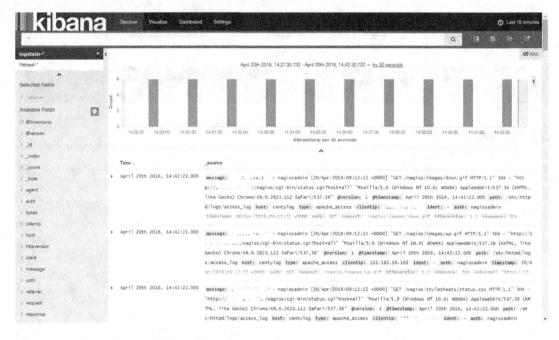

Figure 4-18. *Index patterns displayed*

Click filebeat-*, and you will see the screen shown in Figure 4-19.

Figure 4-19. *Output of filebeat-**

We have now configured the ELK Stack to receive input from remote servers using Filebeat. We can also send the input to Logstash first and then have Logstash send it to Elasticsearch for indexing, or we can send the input directly to Elasticsearch.

Filebeat CLI Flags

You should always check the options that an application provides. Table 4-1 provides a list of all the command-line interface (CLI) flags that Filebeat provides. You can use the --help option, as shown here, to view the CLI flags.

```
vishne0@srv [/root]# sudo filebeat --help
```

Table 4-1. *Filebeat CLI Flags*

Options	Summary
-N	Disable actual publishing for testing
-c string	Configuration file (default /root/filebeat.yml)
-configtest	Test configuration and exit
-cpuprofile string	Write CPU profile to file
-d string	Enable certain debug selectors
-e	Log to stderr and disable syslog/file output
-httpprof string	Start pprof HTTP server
-memprofile string	Write memory profile to this file
-v	Log at INFO level
-version	Print version and exit

Summary

In this chapter, you learned how to install Filebeat on CentOS 7 and Ubuntu servers. I have also taught you how Filebeat can be configured with Logstash and Elasticsearch. You also learned how to do the following:

- Install Filebeat on remote server
- Configure Filebeat to send inputs to Logstash
- Configure Filebeat to send inputs to Elsticsearch
- Configure Kibana to show the indexes from a remote server

In next chapter, you will see how to send inputs from different services, such as Apache, MySQL, e-mail server, Syslog, SSH log, and so on, from a remote server to an ELK Stack.

CHAPTER 5

■ ■ ■

Configuring Logstash for Services and System Logs

In the previous chapter, you learned how to configure Filebeat to send events to a centralized log server. In Chapter 3, you learned how to get events from the Apache access_log to your ELK Stack setup.

Today, almost every company is running multiple servers for their web sites, databases, mobile apps, and so on. We configured the ELK Stack to analyze logs at a central place for our infrastructure, so we have to watch and search all of the events.

In this chapter, you will learn how to configure different types of logs for your ELK Stack setup. Furthermore, you will learn how to configure events from different log files on servers

To begin, first you will send the events from the Syslog to your ELK stack. Syslog is the standard for most Unix-based systems. It stores logs in /var/log/messages.

Syslog Configuration with Logstash CentOS 7

Syslog comes with CentOS 7 by default. Depending on the setup, Syslog can collect messages from various services or programs. You will now configure Logstash to get the events from /var/log/messages.

Create a configuration file in /etc/logstash/conf.d, using the name 05-syslog.conf. The content of the file will be similar to the code shown here:

```
input {
  file {
  path            => "/var/log/messages"
  start_position => beginning
  }
}

output {

elasticsearch {

hosts => ["localhost:9200"]
}
stdout { codec => rubydebug }

}
```

© Vishal Sharma 2016

V. Sharma, *Beginning Elastic Stack*, DOI 10.1007/978-1-4842-1694-1_5

In Figure 5-1, we followed the same pattern as with other configuration files in earlier chapters. In the input section, we are using a `file` variable and the path for `/var/log/messages`. In the output section, we are sending it to Elasticsearch as a simple configuration. The most important thing to remember here is that `/var/log/messages` is owned by root, and it doesn't allow permission for any other users to read the file. You must have Logstash `user` allow permission to read the `/var/log/messages` file. To do this, run the following simple command:

```
[vishneo@snf-718079 log]$ sudo setfacl -m u:logstash:r /var/log/messages
```

```
input {
  file {
    path             => "/var/ log/messages"
    start_position => beginning
  }
}

output {

elasticsearch {

hosts => ["localhost:9200"]
}
stdout { codec => rubydebug }

}
```

Figure 5-1. *Configuring Logstash to receive events from* `/var/log/messages`

And that's it, really. As you have already configured Kibana, you can check if you are seeing the events from `/var/log/messages`.

As you can see in Figure 5-2, Kibana is now showing events from `/var/log/messages`. Thus, we now have our Syslog events configured on CentOS 7.

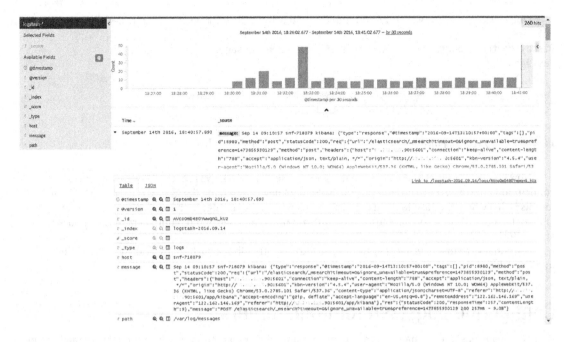

Figure 5-2. Logs in Kibana for `/var/log/messages`

Syslog Configuration with Logstash on Ubuntu 16.04.1 LTS

On Ubuntu minimal Syslog is not installed by default. Thus, first, you have to install the Syslog package on your Ubuntu machine (Figure 5-3). Remember, before installing anything on a freshly installed server, always check to see if any updates are available.

```
vishal_gnutech@ubuntu-xenial-1:/$ sudo apt-get update
vishal_gnutech@ubuntu-xenial-1:/$ sudo apt-get upgrade
vishal_gnutech@ubuntu-xenial-1:/$ sudo apt-get install syslog-ng
Type 'Y'
```

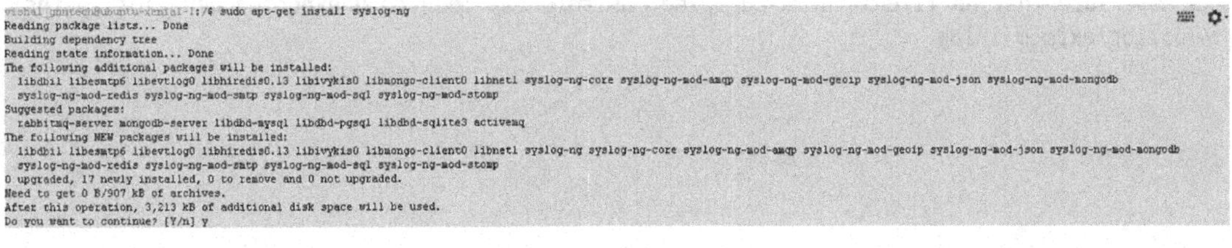

Figure 5-3. Installing `syslog-ng` on Ubuntu 16.04.1 LTS

Once installed, go to /var/log/ and run 'ls'. You will see the file messages (Figure 5-4):

```
vishal_gnutech@ubuntu-xenial-1:/var/log$ ls | grep messages
messages
```

```
vishal_gnutech@ubuntu-xenial-1:/var/log$ ls | grep messages
messages
```

Figure 5-4. syslog-ng *installed and created the file messages in* /var/log

Now copy the content of the file from the previous section of 05-syslog.conf and create a new configuration file in /etc/logstash/conf.d. Note that I have named the file 05-syslog.conf. The reason for this is that when Logstash looks at a directory, in our case, /etc/logstash/conf.d, it loads files in alphabetic order. Thus, if you have too many configuration files, you should name them properly, to avoid any confusion.

Once that's complete, restart Logstash, then log on to the Kibana dashboard, and you will see the incoming data.

Configuring Logstash for Mail Servers

Every company has its own mail servers. There are things that a server admin must monitor on a mail server daily, such as incoming spam, suspicious files sent as attachments, mail delivery failure, and so forth. You will be learning about two of the most commonly used e-mail solutions on GNU/Linux servers Exim and Postfix. You will learn, too, how to configure Logstash for these e-mail server programs.

To proceed, we must assume that at least one of the e-mail server software programs is already installed.

Exim Configuration

Exim is a mail transfer agent mostly used with cPanel and Mailman. Exim both logs and saves the logs in /var/log/exim/mainlog. If you have a server running cPanel, then the log files will be located at /var/log/. You will now see how to configure Exim logs with Logstash. I am assuming that the mail server is a remote server. To send the logs from a remote mail server to your ELK Stack, you will configure Filebeat, as explained in Chapter 4, and make the changes in /etc/filebeat.yml, as shown here (Figure 5-5):

```
  # Make sure that no file is defined twice, as this can lead to unexpected behavior. paths:
- /var/log/exim_mainlog
```

```
################### Filebeat Configuration Example ########################

############################# Filebeat ###################################
filebeat:
  # List of prospectors to fetch data.
  prospectors:
    # Each - is a prospector. Below are the prospector specific configurations
      -
      # Paths that should be crawled and fetched. Glob based paths.
      # To fetch all ".log" files from a specific level of subdirectories
      # /var/log/*/*.log can be used.
      # For each file found under this path, a harvester is started.
      # Make sure not file is defined twice as this can lead to unexpected behaviour.
      paths:
        - /var/log/exim_mainlog
        #- c:\programdata\elasticsearch\logs\*
```

Figure 5-5. *Configuring* `filebeat.yml` *to read Exim logs*

As shown in Figure 5-5, we have configured Filebeat to read Exim logs. In some cases, you might have logs located in /var/log/exim/. Make sure that you have opened port 5044 in the firewall.

Once that's done, save it and restart Filebeat. Now let's check Kibana, to see if we are getting the events. Open the Kibana dashboard and check `logstash-*` index.

Figure 5-6 reveals that your ELK Stack is getting events from the remote mail server, and it shows you the logs. Exim also produces a panic log and reject logs as well. You can also configure them in `filebeat.yml`. Set their path as /var/log/exim/*.log, or define them each in a single line, as follows:

```
# Make sure that no file is defined twice, as this can lead to unexpected behavior.
    paths:
        - /var/log/exim_mainlog
        - /var/log/exim_rejectlog
        - /var/log/exim_painclog
```

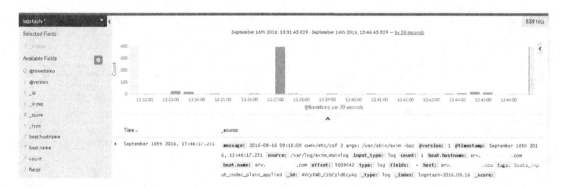

Figure 5-6. *Kibana showing Exim logs from the remote server*

Postfix Configuration

Postfix is one of the most popular and widely used mail servers in the world. It runs on all available Unix systems. Postfix saves the log file at /var/log/maillog.

You will now configure your Postfix-based mail server to send events to the ELK Stack (Figure 5-7). As described in Chapter 4, install Filebeat on the mail server and change the filebeat.yml file as described here:

```
# Make sure that no file is defined twice, as this can lead to unexpected behavior.
      paths:
              - /var/log/maillog
```

```
# Paths that should be crawled and fetched. Glob based paths.
# To fetch all ".log" files from a specific level of subdirectories
# /var/log/*/*.log can be used.
# For each file found under this path, a harvester is started.
# Make sure not file is defined twice as this can lead to unexpected behaviour.
paths:
  - /var/log/maillog
  #- c:\programdata\elasticsearch\logs\*
```

Figure 5-7. *Configuring logs for Postfix in Filebeat*

Restart Filebeat. Now check your Kibana dashboard to see if you are getting the events.

As you can see in Figure 5-8, Postfix logs are now coming to the Kibana dashboard.

Figure 5-8. *Postfix events in the Kibana dashboard*

Configuring Secure Log

It's very important for every server administrator to keep an eye on the logs, for authentication and authorization privileges. In GNU/Linux systems, you have a log file for that: /var/log/secure. The log file contains information about successful accesses as well as failed ones. You can analyze the log and block an attacker's IP.

We will now configure secure logs. As you have seen in earlier sections, we will be using Filebeat to allow remote servers to send events to our ELK Stack. You have to install Filebeat on every remote server from which you want to receive events. (Refer to Chapter 4 for how to install and configure Filebeat.) Once Filebeat is installed, open /etc/filebeat/filebeat.yml and make the following changes:

```
  -
    # Paths that should be crawled and fetched. Glob based paths.
    # To fetch all ".log" files from a specific level of subdirectories
    # /var/log/*/*.log can be used.
    # For each file found under this path, a harvester is started.
    # Make sure not file is defined twice as this can lead to unexpected behavior.
    paths:
      - /var/log/secure
```

As shown in Figure 5-9, you have configured Filebeat to read the /var/log/secure file. Now check Kibana for events coming in from /var/log/secure.

```
# Each - is a prospector. Below are the prospector specific configurations
  -
  # Paths that should be crawled and fetched. Glob based paths.
  # To fetch all ".log" files from a specific level of subdirectories
  # /var/log/*/*.log can be used.
  # For each file found under this path, a harvester is started.
  # Make sure not file is defined twice as this can lead to unexpected behaviour.
  paths:
    ▪ /var/log/secure
```

Figure 5-9. *Configuring Filebeat for /var/log/secure*

As shown in Figure 5-10, you can see such details as the IP address and the username of the failed authentication. This kind of information is very useful to server administrators. You can use this information to make your servers more secure, by blocking an attacker's IP.

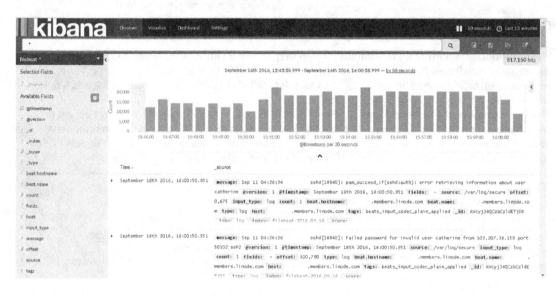

Figure 5-10. Secure log content from the remote server

MySQL Logs

MySQL is an open source relational database management system that is used worldwide. Database log monitoring is very important, as you can identify errors or queries that are slowing your application, and a lot more. Install Filebeat on a remote server, as explained in Chapter 4. Now, before you move forward and configure Filebeat, you must configure MySQL to generate a slow log. Open the MySQL configuration file, as follows (see also Figure 5-11):

```
[vishne0@centylog log]$ sudo  vi /etc/my.cnf
[mysqld]
datadir=/var/lib/mysql
socket=/var/lib/mysql/mysql.sock
user=mysql
# Disabling symbolic-links is recommended to prevent assorted security risks
symbolic-links=0
secure-file-priv=/var/tmp
log-slow-queries=/var/lib/mysql/slow.log
[mysqld_safe]
log-error=/var/log/mysqld.log
pid-file=/var/run/mysqld/mysqld.pid
```

```
[mysqld]
datadir=/var/lib/mysql
socket=/var/lib/mysql/mysql.sock
user=mysql
# Disabling symbolic-links is recommended to prevent assorted security risks
symbolic-links=0
secure-file-priv=/var/tmp
log-slow-queries=/var/lib/mysql/slow.log
[mysqld_safe]
log-error=/var/log/mysqld.log
pid-file=/var/run/mysqld/mysqld.pid
~
~
```

Figure 5-11. *Configuring a MySQL slow log*

As shown in Figure 5-11, a line is added to my.cnf to enable a slow-queries log. Now restart the MySQL server, as follows:

```
[vishne0@centylog log]$ sudo service mysql restart
```

Check to see if the file is created.

```
[vishne0@centylog log]$ cd /var/lib/mysql/
[vishne0@centylog log]$ ls | grep slow
slow.log
```

The file is created, so let's move forward and configure Filebeat. Open the file /etc/filebeat/filebeat.yml in an editor.

```
[vishne0@centylog log]$ sudo vi /etc/filebeat/filebeat.yml
```

```
# Make sure that no file is defined twice, as this can lead to unexpected behavior.
      paths:
              - /var/lib/mysql/slow.log
```

As shown in Figure 5-12, you have configured Filebeat to read the MySQL slow query log file. Save the file and restart Filebeat, as follows:

```
[vishne0@centylog log]$ sudo service filebeat restart
```

```
# Paths that should be crawled and fetched. Glob based paths.
# To fetch all ".log" files from a specific level of subdirectories
# /var/log/*/*.log can be used.
# For each file found under this path, a harvester is started.
# Make sure not file is defined twice as this can lead to unexpected behaviour.
paths:
  - /var/lib/mysql/slow.log
```

Figure 5-12. *Configuring Filebeat to read the MySQL slow log*

Your job is done here. Open the Kibana dashboard and see if you are receiving the inputs. Always remember that you must open port 5044 on every server on which you are configuring Filebeat.

As shown in Figure 5-13, we are about to view a query that is taking a long time to execute.

The preceding are just a few examples of logs that you can configure using Filebeat and Logstash. There are lots of other kinds of logs, such as audit.log, which can be configured, as well as any other application running on a remote server that you want to configure.

Figure 5-13. *Logs of MySQL slow query*

Summary

In this chapter, you learned how to configure system and services logs using Filebeat on your ELK Stack. You also learned the following:

- How to allow permission to Logstash user to read files

- How to configure mail logs from Exim and Postfix

- How to configure a MySQL slow log query

Thus far, we have configured our ELK Stack and have also configured events from a remote server. With this and previous chapters, the most basic and important aspects of the ELK Stack have now been covered.

In next chapter, you will see how to configure Graphite with the ELK Stack, to monitor and analyze historical logs and data.

CHAPTER 6

■ ■ ■

Graphite Monitoring and Graphs

In previous chapters, you learned how to set up an ELK Stack and use the web-based interface Kibana to see the events from the data received by Logstash and Elasticsearch. You also configured remote hosts to send inputs to a centralized ELK Stack. Now a monitoring system keeps running for a longer period of time, and it keeps getting data from the services or server it's monitoring. Monitoring systems generally don't possess the functionality for long-term data analysis and storage. Fortunately, you can use Graphite with the ELK Stack, to gain more control over how you analyze your historical logs and data.

In this chapter, you will learn how to install and use Graphite and its components on CentOS 7 and Ubuntu 16.04.1 LTS systems with data input from Elasticsearch.

Installing Graphite on CentOS 7

You will install Graphite along with its three components:

1. *Carbon*: A daemon listens for time-series data.

2. *Whisper*: A database similar to RRD tools provides storage for numeric time-series data.

3. *Graphite-web*: Renders graphs and provides a visualization and analysis of the data.

Preinstallation Setup

The first thing to do on a freshly installed server is to check to see if any updates are available. If there are any updates, install them immediately, to be sure that your server is up to date.

```
[vishne0@localhost ~]$ sudo yum check-update
[vishne0@localhost ~]$ sudo yum update
```

Now all that is needed is to enable the EPEL repository for your CentOS 7. Let's do it as follows:

```
[vishne0@localhost ~]$ sudo yum install epel-release
```

© Vishal Sharma 2016

V. Sharma, *Beginning Elastic Stack*, DOI 10.1007/978-1-4842-1694-1_6

As shown in Figure 6-1, the EPEL repository is now installed.

```
[vishne0@localhost ~]$ sudo yum install epel-release
[sudo] password for vishne0:
Loaded plugins: fastestmirror
Loading mirror speeds from cached hostfile
 * base: mirrors.linode.com
 * extras: mirrors.linode.com
 * updates: mirrors.linode.com
Resolving Dependencies
--> Running transaction check
---> Package epel-release.noarch 0:7-6 will be installed
--> Finished Dependency Resolution

Dependencies Resolved

================================================================================
 Package              Arch           Version          Repository         Size
================================================================================
Installing:
 epel-release         noarch         7-6              extras             14 k

Transaction Summary
================================================================================
Install  1 Package

Total download size: 14 k
Installed size: 24 k
Is this ok [y/d/N]: y
Downloading packages:
epel-release-7-6.noarch.rpm                                |  14 kB  00:00:00
Running transaction check
Running transaction test
Transaction test succeeded
Running transaction
  Installing : epel-release-7-6.noarch                                     1/1
  Verifying  : epel-release-7-6.noarch                                     1/1

Installed:
  epel-release.noarch 0:7-6

Complete!
[vishne0@localhost ~]$
```

Figure 6-1. *Installing the EPEL repository on CentOS 7*

Installing Graphite on CentOS 7

Now it's time to install Graphite, in addition to the required packages. Enter the following command:

```
[vishne0@centylog opt]$ sudo yum install pycairo django bitmap bitmap-fonts mod_wsgi python-pip python-devel gcc httpd
```

The preceding dependencies are installed according to the package requirement form on the Graphite web site at http://graphite.wikidot.com/installation.

As shown in Figure 6-2, all the packages and dependencies are installed. Now we will use PIP, which is a package management system used to install and manage Python packages. To move ahead, we will first upgrade PIP, as follows:

```
[vishne0@localhost ~]$ sudo pip install --upgrade pip
[vishne0@localhost ~]$ sudo pip install carbon
[vishne0@localhost ~]$ sudo pip install whisper
[vishne0@localhost ~]$ sudo pip install graphite-web
[vishne0@localhost ~]$ sudo pip install "django-tagging<0.4"
```

```
Verifying  : pycairo-1.8.10-8.el7.x86_64                                                                          35/52
Verifying  : libXt-1.1.4-6.1.el7.x86_64                                                                           36/52
Verifying  : libxshmfence-1.2-1.el7.x86_64                                                                        37/52
Verifying  : mesa-libglapi-10.6.5-3.20150824.el7.x86_64                                                           38/52
Verifying  : libXfixes-5.0.1-2.1.el7.x86_64                                                                       39/52
Verifying  : cpp-4.8.5-4.el7.x86_64                                                                               40/52
Verifying  : httpd-tools-2.4.6-40.el7.centos.4.x86_64                                                             41/52
Verifying  : cairo-1.14.2-1.el7.x86_64                                                                            42/52
Verifying  : mpfr-3.1.1-4.el7.x86_64                                                                              43/52
Verifying  : fontconfig-2.10.95-7.el7.x86_64                                                                      44/52
Verifying  : libxcb-1.11-4.el7.x86_64                                                                             45/52
Verifying  : libXau-1.0.8-2.1.el7.x86_64                                                                          46/52
Verifying  : mesa-libGL-10.6.5-3.20150824.el7.x86_64                                                              47/52
Verifying  : xorg-x11-xbitmaps-1.1.1-6.el7.noarch                                                                 48/52
Verifying  : libXdamage-1.1.4-4.1.el7.x86_64                                                                      49/52
Verifying  : mesa-libEGL-10.6.5-3.20150824.el7.x86_64                                                             50/52
Verifying  : bitmap-lucida-typewriter-fonts-0.3-21.el7.noarch                                                     51/52
Verifying  : python-django-bash-completion-1.6.11-5.el7.noarch                                                    52/52

Installed:
  bitmap.x86_64 0:1.0.7-4.el7           bitmap-fonts-compat.noarch 0:0.3-21.el7     gcc.x86_64 0:4.8.5-4.el7        httpd.x86_64 0:2.4.6-40.el7.centos.4
  mod_wsgi.x86_64 0:3.4-12.el7_0        pycairo.x86_64 0:1.8.10-8.el7               python-devel.x86_64 0:2.7.5-39.el7_2    python-django.noarch 0:1.6.11-5.el7
  python-pip.noarch 0:7.1.0-1.el7

Dependency Installed:
  apr.x86_64 0:1.4.8-3.el7                    apr-util.x86_64 0:1.5.2-6.el7               bitmap-console-fonts.noarch 0:0.3-21.el7
  bitmap-fangsongti-fonts.noarch 0:0.3-21.el7  bitmap-fixed-fonts.noarch 0:0.3-21.el7     bitmap-lucida-typewriter-fonts.noarch 0:0.3-21.el7
  cairo.x86_64 0:1.14.2-1.el7                 cpp.x86_64 0:4.8.5-4.el7                    fontconfig.x86_64 0:2.10.95-7.el7
  fontpackages-filesystem.noarch 0:1.44-6.el7/  freetype.x86_64 0:2.4.11-11.el7          glibc-devel.x86_64 0:2.17-106.el7_2.8
  glibc-headers.x86_64 0:2.17-106.el7_2.8     httpd-tools.x86_64 0:2.4.6-40.el7.centos.4  kernel-headers.x86_64 0:3.10.0-327.36.1.el7
  libICE.x86_64 0:1.0.9-2.el7                 libSM.x86_64 0:1.2.2-2.el7                  libX11.x86_64 0:1.6.3-2.el7
  libX11-common.noarch 0:1.6.3-2.el7          libXau.x86_64 0:1.0.8-2.1.el7              libXaw.x86_64 0:1.0.12-5.el7
  libXdamage.x86_64 0:1.1.4-4.1.el7           libXext.x86_64 0:1.3.3-3.el7               libXfixes.x86_64 0:5.0.1-2.1.el7
  libXmu.x86_64 0:1.1.2-2.el7                 libXpm.x86_64 0:3.5.11-3.el7               libXrender.x86_64 0:0.9.8-2.1.el7
  libXt.x86_64 0:1.1.4-6.1.el7                libXxf86vm.x86_64 0:1.1.3-2.1.el7          libpc.x86_64 0:1.0.1-3.el7
  libpng.x86_64 2:1.5.13-7.el7_2              libxcb.x86_64 0:1.11-4.el7                 libxshmfence.x86_64 0:1.2-1.el7
  mailcap.noarch 0:2.1.41-2.el7              mesa-libEGL.x86_64 0:10.6.5-3.20150824.el7  mesa-libGL.x86_64 0:10.6.5-3.20150824.el7
  mesa-libgbm.x86_64 0:10.6.5-3.20150824.el7  mesa-libglapi.x86_64 0:10.6.5-3.20150824.el7  mpfr.x86_64 0:3.1.1-4.el7
  pixman.x86_64 0:0.32.6-3.el7               python-django-bash-completion.noarch 0:1.6.11-5.el7  ucs-miscfixed-fonts.noarch 0:0.3-11.el7
  xorg-x11-xbitmaps.noarch 0:1.1.1-6.el7

Complete!
[vishne0@localhost ~]$
[vishne0@localhost ~]$ █
```

Figure 6-2. *Installing dependencies for Graphite*

In the preceding command, we are installing an earlier version of django-tagging than the latest, which is 0.4.5 at the time of writing. The reason that we are installing an earlier version is that in later sections, we will be generating the database and user for the Graphite database, and it will not work with the newer version of django-tagging.

Now that all of the required packages are installed, we can configure Graphite, Carbon, Whisper, and Graphite-web.

Configuring Graphite, Carbon, and Whisper

All of the packages needed on our CentOS 7 server are now installed. Next, we will configure Graphite, Carbon, and Whisper.

```
[vishne0@centylog /]$ cd /opt/graphite/conf/
```

Next, copy carbon.conf.example to carbon.conf:

```
[vishne0@localhost conf]$ sudo cp carbon.conf.example carbon.conf
```

Now open the file carbon.conf and explore its options (Figure 6-3):

```
[vishne0@centylog conf]$ sudo vi carbon.conf
```

```
[cache]
# Configure carbon directories.
#
# OS environment variables can be used to tell carbon where graphite is
# installed, where to read configuration from and where to write data.
#
#   GRAPHITE_ROOT        - Root directory of the graphite installation.
#                          Defaults to ../
#   GRAPHITE_CONF_DIR    - Configuration directory (where this file lives).
#                          Defaults to $GRAPHITE_ROOT/conf/
#   GRAPHITE_STORAGE_DIR - Storage directory for whisper/rrd/log/pid files.
#                          Defaults to $GRAPHITE_ROOT/storage/
#
# To change other directory paths, add settings to this file. The following
# configuration variables are available with these default values:
#
#   STORAGE_DIR      = $GRAPHITE_STORAGE_DIR
#   LOCAL_DATA_DIR   = STORAGE_DIR/whisper/
#   WHITELISTS_DIR   = STORAGE_DIR/lists/
#   CONF_DIR         = STORAGE_DIR/conf/
#   LOG_DIR          = STORAGE_DIR/log/
#   PID_DIR          = STORAGE_DIR/
#
# For FHS style directory structures, use:
#
#   STORAGE_DIR      = /var/lib/carbon/
#   CONF_DIR         = /etc/carbon/
#   LOG_DIR          = /var/log/carbon/
#   PID_DIR          = /var/run/
#
#LOCAL_DATA_DIR = /opt/graphite/storage/whisper/

# Enable daily log rotation. If disabled, carbon will automatically re-open
# the file if it's rotated out of place (e.g. by logrotate daemon)
ENABLE_LOGROTATION = True

# Specify the user to drop privileges to
# If this is blank carbon runs as the user that invokes it
# This user must have write access to the local data directory
USER =
#
# NOTE: The above settings must be set under [relay] and [aggregator]
#       to take effect for those daemons as well
"carbon.conf" 402L, 17809C
```

Figure 6-3. *Configuring carbon.conf*

You can normally examine the settings here and make changes, if needed, to your setup. However, we will leave the carbon.conf file untouched and use the default settings. Now let's move on to configure the storage schemas.

Copy storage-schemas.conf.example to storage-schemas.conf, as follows:

```
[vishne0@localhost conf]$ sudo cp storage-schemas.conf.example storage-schemas.conf
```

Edit the file, as follows:

```
[vishne0@centylog conf]$ sudo vi storage-schemas.conf
# Schema definitions for Whisper files. Entries are scanned in order,
# and first match wins. This file is scanned for changes every 60 seconds.
#
```

```
#   [name]
#   pattern = regex
#   retentions = timePerPoint:timeToStore, timePerPoint:timeToStore, ...

# Carbon's internal metrics. This entry should match what is specified in
# CARBON_METRIC_PREFIX and CARBON_METRIC_INTERVAL settings
[carbon]
pattern = ^carbon\.
retentions = 60:90d

[default_1min_for_1day]
pattern = .*
retentions = 60s:1d
```

You will see that there are two sections in the configuration file that contain the following:

- Name of the section

- Field pattern containing regular expressions

- Retention containing values. For example, in the configuration file, retentions= 60s:1d means that the data point represents 60 seconds, and it will be retained for 1 day.

Adding Carbon As a Service on CentOS 7

Copy the init scripts to /etc/init.d/. Change the directory to /opt/graphite, and issue the following commands:

```
[vishne0@localhost graphite]$ sudo cp /opt/graphite/examples/init.d/carbon-* /etc/init.d/
```

Now make the scripts executable with the following command:

```
[vishne0@centylog graphite]$ sudo chmod +x /etc/init.d/carbon-*
```

Start carbon-cache, as follows:

```
[vishne0@localhost graphite]$ sudo /etc/init.d/carbon-cache start
Reloading systemd:                                      [  OK  ]
Starting carbon-cache (via systemctl):                  [  OK  ]
```

Now check to see if it's running (Figure 6-4):

```
[vishne0@localhost graphite]$ sudo /etc/init.d/carbon-cache status
carbon-cache (instance a) is running with pid 18932
                                                        [  OK  ]
```

Figure 6-4. Starting Carbon and checking that it's running properly

As you can see in Figure 6-4, Carbon is running and will receive the data, which means that it is configured properly.

Configuring Graphite-web

Graphite-web is a Django-based application that displays graphs and dashboards. Now it's time to configure Graphite-web. First copy the following sample configuration file:

[vishne0@localhost graphite]$ sudo cp /opt/graphite/webapp/graphite/local_settings.
py.example /opt/graphite/webapp/graphite/local_settings.py

To edit the file, issue the following command (Figure 6-5):

[vishne0@centylog graphite]$ sudo vi /opt/graphite/webapp/graphite/local_settings.py

```
# Graphite local_settings.py
# Edit this file to customize the default Graphite webapp settings
#
# Additional customizations to Django settings can be added to this file as well

#####################################
# General Configuration #
#####################################
# Set this to a long, random unique string to use as a secret key for this
# install. This key is used for salting of hashes used in auth tokens,
# CRSF middleware, cookie storage, etc. This should be set identically among
# instances if used behind a load balancer.
#SECRET_KEY = 'UNSAFE_DEFAULT'

# In Django 1.5+ set this to the list of hosts your graphite instances is
# accessible as. See:
# https://docs.djangoproject.com/en/dev/ref/settings/#std:setting-ALLOWED_HOSTS
#ALLOWED_HOSTS = [ '*' ]

# Set your local timezone (Django's default is America/Chicago)
# If your graphs appear to be offset by a couple hours then this probably
# needs to be explicitly set to your local timezone.
#TIME_ZONE = 'America/Los_Angeles'

# Override this to provide documentation specific to your Graphite deployment
#DOCUMENTATION_URL = "http://graphite.readthedocs.org/"

# Logging
#LOG_RENDERING_PERFORMANCE = True
#LOG_CACHE_PERFORMANCE = True
#LOG_METRIC_ACCESS = True

# Enable full debug page display on exceptions (Internal Server Error pages)
#DEBUG = True

# If using RRD files and rrdcached, set to the address or socket of the daemon
#FLUSHRRDCACHED = 'unix:/var/run/rrdcached.sock'

# This lists the memcached servers that will be used by this webapp.
# If you have a cluster of webapps you should ensure all of them
# have the *exact* same value for this setting. That will maximize cache
# efficiency. Setting MEMCACHE_HOSTS to be empty will turn off use of
# memcached entirely.
"/opt/graphite/webapp/graphite/local_settings.py" 221L, 9234C
```

Figure 6-5. *Editing the* local_setting.py *for Graphite-web*

As shown in Figure 6-5, you must first provide a secret key. Uncomment the line SECRET_KEY ='' and provide a key. In my case, for testing, I have provided the key J4f4#!9.

Uncomment the Time_Zone= '' and enter your time zone. In my case, I have changed the default to TIME_ZONE = 'UTC'.

Now exit from the editor, by first pressing Esc. Save the file and quit, by pressing :wq (Figure 6-6).

```
# Graphite local_settings.py
# Edit this file to customize the default Graphite webapp settings
#
# Additional customizations to Django settings can be added to this file as well

#####################################
# General Configuration #
#####################################
# Set this to a long, random unique string to use as a secret key for this
# install. This key is used for salting of hashes used in auth tokens,
# CRSF middleware, cookie storage, etc. This should be set identically among
# instances if used behind a load balancer.
SECRET_KEY = 'J4f4#!9'

# In Django 1.5+ set this to the list of hosts your graphite instances is
# accessible as. See:
# https://docs.djangoproject.com/en/dev/ref/settings/#std:setting-ALLOWED_HOSTS
#ALLOWED_HOSTS = [ '*' ]

# Set your local timezone (Django's default is America/Chicago)
# If your graphs appear to be offset by a couple hours then this probably
# needs to be explicitly set to your local timezone.
TIME_ZONE = 'UTC'

# Override this to provide documentation specific to your Graphite deployment
#DOCUMENTATION_URL = "http://graphite.readthedocs.org/"

# Logging
#LOG_RENDERING_PERFORMANCE = True
#LOG_CACHE_PERFORMANCE = True
#LOG_METRIC_ACCESS = True

# Enable full debug page display on exceptions (Internal Server Error pages)
#DEBUG = True

# If using RRD files and rrdcached, set to the address or socket of the daemon
#FLUSHRRDCACHED = 'unix:/var/run/rrdcached.sock'

# This lists the memcached servers that will be used by this webapp.
# If you have a cluster of webapps you should ensure all of them
# have the *exact* same value for this setting. That will maximize cache
# efficiency. Setting MEMCACHE_HOSTS to be empty will turn off use of
# memcached entirely.
```

Figure 6-6. *Editing and saving the* local_setting.py *Graphite-web config file*

Next, you'll set up the Graphite database and user, starting with the following command:

```
[vishne0@centylog graphite]$ sudo python /opt/graphite/webapp/graphite/manage.py syncdb
```

As shown in Figure 6-7, you are prompted to create a superuser. Create the user, and provide the information that is requested. You are now done with installing and configuring Graphite, Carbon, and Whisper. Next, you will configure Graphite to run, using Apache. The Graphite installation comes with sample configuration files. We will change the directory to /opt/graphite/examples.

```
[vishne0@localhost graphite]$ sudo python /opt/graphite/webapp/graphite/manage.py syncdb
Creating tables ...
Creating table account_profile
Creating table account_variable
Creating table account_view
Creating table account_window
Creating table account_mygraph
Creating table dashboard_dashboard_owners
Creating table dashboard_dashboard
Creating table events_event
Creating table url_shortener_link
Creating table auth_permission
Creating table auth_group_permissions
Creating table auth_group
Creating table auth_user_groups
Creating table auth_user_user_permissions
Creating table auth_user
Creating table django_session
Creating table django_admin_log
Creating table django_content_type
Creating table tagging_tag
Creating table tagging_taggeditem

You just installed Django's auth system, which means you don't have any superusers defined.
Would you like to create one now? (yes/no): yes
Username (leave blank to use 'root'): graphitedb
Email address: graphitedb@gmail.com
Password:
Password (again):
Superuser created successfully.
Installing custom SQL ...
Installing indexes ...
Installed 0 object(s) from 0 fixture(s)
[vishne0@localhost graphite]$ 
```

Figure 6-7. *Generating the Graphite database and creating the admin user*

Inside the directory, you will see a file named example-graphite-vhost.conf. Copy it to /etc/httpd/conf.d.

```
[vishne0@centylog graphite]$ cd examples/
[vishne0@localhost examples]$ sudo cp example-graphite-vhost.conf /etc/httpd/conf.d/
graphite.conf
```

The sample files that come with the Graphite installation have everything you need to configure it to run using Apache. Let's see what configuration is needed here. Change the directory to /etc/httpd/conf.d.

```
[vishne0@localhost examples]$ cd /etc/httpd/conf.d/
```

Now open the file using vi.

```
[vishne0@centylog conf.d]$ sudo vi graphite.conf
```

Now let's see all the changes you have to make in graphite.conf (Figure 6-8).

```
# This needs to be in your server's config somewhere, probably
# the main httpd.conf
# NameVirtualHost *:80

# This line also needs to be in your server's config.
# LoadModule wsgi_module modules/mod_wsgi.so

# You need to manually edit this file to fit your needs.
# This configuration assumes the default installation prefix
# of /opt/graphite/, if you installed graphite somewhere else
# you will need to change all the occurances of /opt/graphite/
# in this file to your chosen install location.

<IfModule !wsgi_module.c>
    LoadModule wsgi_module modules/mod_wsgi.so
</IfModule>

# XXX You need to set this up!
# Read http://code.google.com/p/modwsgi/wiki/ConfigurationDirectives#WSGISocketPrefix
WSGISocketPrefix run/wsgi

<VirtualHost *:80>
        ServerName graphite
        DocumentRoot "/opt/graphite/webapp"
        ErrorLog /opt/graphite/storage/log/webapp/error.log
        CustomLog /opt/graphite/storage/log/webapp/access.log common

        # I've found that an equal number of processes & threads tends
        # to show the best performance for Graphite (ymmv).
        WSGIDaemonProcess graphite processes=5 threads=5 display-name='%{GROUP}' inactivity-timeout=120
        WSGIProcessGroup graphite
        WSGIApplicationGroup %{GLOBAL}
        WSGIImportScript /opt/graphite/conf/graphite.wsgi process-group=graphite application-group=%{GLOBAL}

        # XXX You will need to create this file! There is a graphite.wsgi.example
        # file in this directory that you can safely use, just copy it to graphite.wgsi
        WSGIScriptAlias / /opt/graphite/conf/graphite.wsgi

        # XXX To serve static files, either:
        # django-admin.py collectstatic --noinput --settings=graphite.settings
        # * Install the whitenoise Python package (pip install whitenoise)
        # or
        # * Collect static files in a directory by running:
"graphite.conf" [noeol] 67L, 2822C
```

Figure 6-8. *Editing graphite.conf to make it run using Apache*

You need to change few things in your graphite.conf file. We will now proceed to do this step by step.

Look for WSGISocketPrefix and change the run.wsgi to /var/run/httpd/wsgi. The changed parameters are as follows:

```
WSGISocketPrefix /var/run/httpd/wsgi
```

Next is the virtualhost section for Graphite-web. This section is very important, as you need to tell Apache to look for Graphite-web. The virtualhost section looks like the following:

```
<VirtualHost *:8880>
        ServerName   yourserver name or server IP
        DocumentRoot "/opt/graphite/webapp"
        ErrorLog /var/log/httpd/graphite_error.log
        CustomLog /var/log/httpd/graphite_access.log common
```

Put your hostname or IP address in ServerName, as shown in Figure 6-9. This is an important change that you have to make. Scroll down to the WSGIScriptAlias section. There, you will see its setup, as follows:

```
WSGIScriptAlias / /opt/graphite/conf/graphite.wsgi
```

```
<VirtualHost *:8880>
        ServerName 192.168.10.100
        DocumentRoot "/opt/graphite/webapp"
        ErrorLog /opt/graphite/storage/log/webapp/error.log
        CustomLog /opt/graphite/storage/log/webapp/access.log common

        # I've found that an equal number of processes & threads tends
        # to show the best performance for Graphite (ymmv).
        WSGIDaemonProcess graphite processes=5 threads=5 display-name='%{GROUP}' inactivity-timeout=120
        WSGIProcessGroup graphite
        WSGIApplicationGroup %{GLOBAL}
        WSGIImportScript /opt/graphite/conf/graphite.wsgi process-group=graphite application-group=%{GLOBAL}

        # XXX You will need to create this file! There is a graphite.wsgi.example
        # file in this directory that you can safely use, just copy it to graphite.wgsi
        WSGIScriptAlias / /opt/graphite/conf/graphite.wsgi

        # XXX To serve static files, either:
        # django-admin.py collectstatic --noinput --settings=graphite.settings
        # * Install the whitenoise Python package (pip install whitenoise)
        # or
        # * Collect static files in a directory by running:
        #      django-admin.py collectstatic --noinput --settings=graphite.settings
        #    And set an alias to serve static files with Apache:
        Alias /content/ /opt/graphite/webapp/content/
        <Location "/content/">
                SetHandler None
        </Location>

        # XXX In order for the django admin site media to work you
        # must change @DJANGO_ROOT@ to be the path to your django
        # installation, which is probably something like:
        # /usr/lib/python2.6/site-packages/django
        #Alias /media/ "@DJANGO_ROOT@/contrib/admin/media/"
        Alias /media/ "/usr/local/lib/python2.7/dist-packages/django/contrib/admin/media/"
        <Location "/media/">
                SetHandler /usr/lib/python2.7/site-packages/django
        </Location>

        # The graphite.wsgi file has to be accessible by apache. It won't
        # be visible to clients because of the DocumentRoot though.
```

Figure 6-9. *Configuring the* virtualhost *section of* graphite.conf

Open another SSH session to the current server and copy /opt/graphite/conf/graphite.wsgi. example to graphite.wsgi.

```
[vishne0@localhost /]$ cd /opt/graphite/conf/
[vishne0@localhost conf]$ sudo cp graphite.wsgi.example graphite.wsgi
```

Scroll down to the section for django admin, and in Alias /media, add the path to "/usr/local/lib/ python2.7/dist-packages/django/contrib/admin/media/".

```
Alias /media/ "/usr/local/lib/python2.7/dist-packages/django/contrib/admin/media/"
        <Location "/media/">
                SetHandler /usr/lib/python2.7/site-packages/django
        </Location>
```

Next, we move to the section for graphite.wsgi and add "Require all granted" inside <Directory /opt/graphite/conf>. I have commented two other options here:

```
<Directory /opt/graphite/conf/>
            Require all granted
            #Order deny,allow
            #Allow from all
        </Directory>
```

Finally, we will add a few <Directory> directives before </VirtualHost> to allow content from /opt/graphite/webapp/content/.

```
<Directory /opt/graphite/webapp/>
        Require all granted
</Directory>
<Directory /opt/graphite/webapp/content/>
        Require all granted
</Directory>
```

Once finished, press Esc and then :wq, to save the file and exit from the editor.

Now you have to add one line to the httpd.conf file, so that it can listen to port 8880. Before doing that, you must make sure that port 8880 is allowed through the firewall. Add the port to the firewall, as follows:

```
[vishne0@localhost /]$ sudo firewall-cmd --permanent --add-port=8880/tcp
[vishne0@localhost /]$ sudo firewall-cmd --reload
```

Now let's add the port 8880 to httpd.conf.

```
[vishne0@localhost /]$ sudo vi /etc/httpd/conf/httpd.conf
```

Under Listen 80, add another line, as follows:

```
Listen 8880 so it should look like below:
Listen 80
Listen 8880
```

What is accomplished here is the running of another Apache instance on port 8880, so that we can access Graphite on that port. Press Esc and then :wq, to save the file and exit from vi. Now restart the Apache server, as follows:

```
[vishne0@centylog conf.d]$ sudo service httpd restart
```

Before accessing Graphite using your web browser, you have to chown a few files for Apache to access, as follows:

```
[vishne0@localhost /]$ sudo chown apache /opt/graphite/storage/log/webapp/
```

Now you will run the Graphite-web interface. Open a browser and type http://yourip:8880, to see if Graphite-web is running.

As you can see in Figure 6-10, Graphite-web is running. but there is no data. Also, there is a broken image appearing in the middle of the screen. To fix this issue, you have to install pytz, as follows:

```
[vishne0@localhost /]$ sudo yum install pytz
```

Figure 6-10. *Graphite-web console running on port 8880*

Restart httpd.

```
[vishne0@localhost /]$ sudo service httpd restart
```

Now open the browser and type the URL http://yourip:8880.

To check it out, click Metrics ➤ Carbon ➤ agents ➤ localhost_localdomain-a, as I didn't set up a hostname here. If you have a hostname set up, it will show the hostname. It will open the tree. Then click avgUpdateTime, as seen in Figure 6-11.

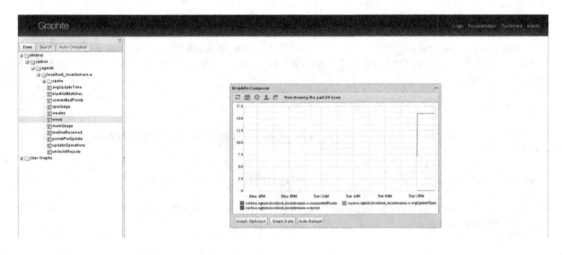

Figure 6-11. *Graphite console showing sample data*

Configuring Logstash to Send Data to Graphite

As you observed in the previous section, Graphite is now installed and configured, and you can see the default data in the graph. However, the ultimate goal is to send the output to Graphite through Logstash. To send the output to Graphite, you will use the Logstash plug-in for Graphite. You may define the Graphite plug-in in your configuration file, as follows:

```
graphite {
}
```

Now let's configure Logstash to send the output to Graphite (Figure 6-12). You will create a new file in your /etc/logstash/conf.d directory named 06-graphitemetrics.conf.

```
[vishne0@localhost conf.d]$ sudo vi 06-graphitemetrics.conf
input {
    file {
        path => "/var/log/httpd/access_log"
    }
}

filter {
    grok {
        match => { "message" => "%{COMBINEDAPACHELOG}" }
    }
    date {
        match => [ "timestamp" , "dd/MMM/yyyy:HH:mm:ss Z" ]
    }

    if [response] =~ /\d\d\d/ {
        metrics {
            meter => "apache.response.%{host}.%{response}"
            add_tag => "metric"
            clear_interval => "5"
            flush_interval => "5"
        }
    }
}

output {
    graphite {
        fields_are_metrics => true
        include_metrics => ["^apache\.response\..*"]
        host => "localhost"
        port => "2003"
    }
stdout {codec => rubydebug }
        }
```

```
input {
    file {
        path => "/var/log/httpd/access_log"
    }
}

filter {
    grok {
        match => { "message" => "%{COMBINEDAPACHELOG}" }
    }
    date {
        match => [ "timestamp" , "dd/MMM/yyyy:HH:mm:ss Z" ]
    }

    if [response] =~ /\d\d\d/ {
        metrics {
            meter => "apache.response.%{host}.%{response}"
            add_tag => "metric"
            clear_interval => "5"
            flush_interval => "5"
        }
    }
}

output {
    graphite {
        fields_are_metrics => true
        include_metrics => ["^apache\.response\..*"]
        host => "localhost"
        port => "2003"
    }
stdout { codec => rubydebug }
}
```

Figure 6-12. *Configuring Logstash to send output to Graphite*

There are several important things to note here. First, I've used Logstash plug-in metrics. We have an http response code and have added a tag, as well, to identify and look for it. Then we are flushing it in every five seconds. Next, we introduce the Logstash plug-in to Graphite. We include the metrics and provide the host and port number for carbon-cache.

Before restarting the services, you should always check to see if your Logstash configuration is correct, so let's run the test.

```
[vishneo@localhost /]$ sudo service logstash configtest
```

If you see Configuration OK, then all is well. Also, you have to make sure that Logstash user has permission to read the /var/log/httpd/access_log.

```
[vishneo@localhost /]$ sudo setfacl -m u:logstash:r /var/log/httpd/access_log
```

```
[vishne0@localhost /]$ sudo service logstash restart
[vishne0@localhost /]$ sudo /etc/init.d/carbon-cache restart
```

Now it's time to check if you are getting any data in Graphite. Point your browser to http://yourip:8880. At the top left, you will see Metrics. Expand it by clicking the Metrics folder. Under that, you will see a new folder with the name apache. Click that folder, and then you will see response ➤ hostname. Under that, you will see folders with the response code. You can see the graphs by clicking the response code folder and then the entries inside that. There are a few important things to note here.

- You should have a busy web site that is sending access logs to your access_log file.

- Make sure that Logstash user has permission to read the file, which I mentioned in an earlier section.

As shown in the Figure 6-13, you are now getting the graphs in Graphite through Logstash. You can see all of the graphs displayed on a single screen. How is that done? Click Dashboard at the top right, then click apache, and keep clicking it until you see the name ending with a response code, such as 200,304,400, and so on. Click apache.response.hostname.200, and you will see the options for count, rate at 1m, 15m, and 5m.

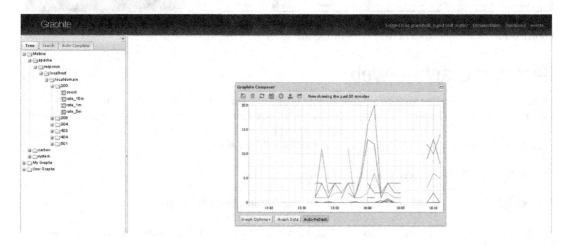

Figure 6-13. *Graphite interface showing graph for count 200*

It's time to rejoice that you are seeing the graphs in Graphite (Figure 6-14). You can do many things with Graphite, including monitoring of the system load, RAM load, and processor load, and comparing the results. A combination of ELK Stack and Graphite is an excellent option for server administrators.

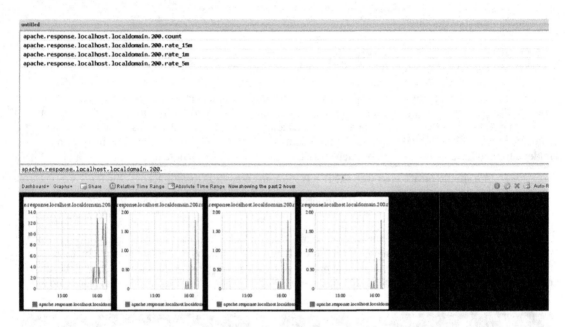

Figure 6-14. *Showing graphs in Graphite dashboard*

Securing Graphite-web

As we are running Graphite-web on a public IP, it's very important to have some type of security. Thus, we will configure a simple http-based authentication. Let's first create a directory in /opt/graphite, as follows:

```
[vishne0@localhost graphite]$ sudo mkdir /opt/graphite/auth
```

We have set the folder, now let's give permission to Apache.

```
[vishne0@localhost graphite]$ sudo chown -R apache:apache /opt/graphite/auth
```

We will use htpasswd to create a new user and give it a password to secure Graphite-web. Let's create the user, as follows:

```
[vishne0@localhost graphite]$ sudo htpasswd -c /opt/graphite/auth/.passwd admgraphite
New password:
Re-type new password:
Adding password for user admgraphite
```

Now you have to configure Apache. Open sudo vi /etc/httpd/conf.d/graphite.conf.

```
[vishne0@localhost graphite]$ sudo vi /etc/httpd/conf.d/graphite.conf
```

In the graphite.conf file, add the following code at the end of the file, just before </VirtualHost>:

```
<Location "/">
    AuthType Basic
    AuthName "Private Area"
```

```
    AuthUserFile /opt/graphite/auth/.passwd
    Require user admgraphite
</Location>
```

Press :wq to save and exit vi. Restart Apache.

```
[vishne0@localhost graphite]$ sudo service httpd restart
```

Your Graphite-web installation is now secure. When you open your browser and point it to your Graphite-web URL, it will ask for username/password.

Installing Graphite on Ubuntu 16.04.1 LTS

In earlier sections, we installed and configured Graphite, Carbon, and Whisper on CentOS 7. Now we will install it on Ubuntu 16.04.1 LTS.

Always update your repository and the system, if updates for packages are available. To accomplish this, run the following command:

```
vishne0@ubuntu:~$ sudo apt-get update && sudo apt-get upgrade
```

Once the upgrades are complete, install the packages you need. I am including Apache2 as well, assuming that it's a fresh Ubuntu installation.

```
vishne0@ubuntu:~$ sudo apt-get install build-essential graphite-web graphite-carbon python-
dev libapache2-mod-wsgi libpq-dev python-psycopg2 apache2
```

While installing the packages, you will see a prompt asking:

The /var/lib/graphite/whisper directory contains the Whisper database files. You may want to keep these database files even if you completely remove graphite-carbon, in case you plan to reinstall it later. Remove database files when purging graphite-carbon. Respond to this prompt with No.

Once the installation is complete and you have everything installed, you must configure it on the Ubuntu server. First, let's configure Carbon. In Ubuntu 16.04.1 LTS, the Carbon configuration files are located in /etc/carbon. The default settings are good enough for us to move ahead and configure Graphite. Before doing that, however, add carbon-cache to boot.

```
vishne0@ubuntu:~$ sudo vi /etc/default/graphite-carbon
```

Change CARBON_CACHE_ENABLED=false to CARBON_CACHE_ENABLED=true. That's it. Start the carbon-cache services, as follows:

```
vishne0@ubuntu:/etc/carbon$ sudo service carbon-cache start
```

Verify that it is running.

```
vishne0@ubuntu:/$ sudo service carbon-cache status
carbon-cache.service - Graphite Carbon Cache
   Loaded: loaded (/lib/systemd/system/carbon-cache.service; enabled; vendor preset:
   enabled)
   Active: active (running) since Mon 2016-10-10 14:21:37 UTC; 9min ago
```

```
 Main PID: 11740 (carbon-cache)
   CGroup: /system.slice/carbon-cache.service
           └─11740 /usr/bin/python /usr/bin/carbon-cache --config=/etc/carbon/carbon.conf
--pidfile=/var/run/carbon-cache.pid --logdir=/var/log/carbon/ start

Oct 10 14:21:37 ubuntu systemd[1]: Starting Graphite Carbon Cache...
Oct 10 14:21:37 ubuntu systemd[1]: Started Graphite Carbon Cache.
Oct 10 14:28:34 ubuntu systemd[1]: Started Graphite Carbon Cache.
```

Now that it's running, it's time to configure Graphite. Enter the following commands:

```
vishne0@ubuntu:/$ cd /etc/graphite/
vishne0@ubuntu:/etc/graphite$ sudo vi local_settings.py
```

In this file, change a few settings. For example, I have changed time zone to UTC.

```
TIME_ZONE = 'UTC'
```

Now make sure the following are uncommented:

```
LOG_RENDERING_PERFORMANCE = True
LOG_CACHE_PERFORMANCE = True
LOG_METRIC_ACCESS = True
```

That's all there is to it!

Configuring Graphite-web

In Ubuntu, you have to copy the configuration files to /etc/apache2/sites-available.

```
vishne0@ubuntu:/$ cd /usr/share/graphite-web/
vishne0@ubuntu:/usr/share/graphite-web$ sudo cp apache2-graphite.conf /etc/apache2/sites-
available/
vishne0@ubuntu:/usr/share/graphite-web$ cd /etc/apache2/sites-available/

vishne0@ubuntu:/etc/apache2/sites-available$ sudo vi apache2-graphite.conf
```

Change the port to 8880 and press :wq to save and exit the vi editor. You will access Graphite on that port. To do this, you have to add port 8880 in the Apache config file, as follows:

```
vishne0@ubuntu:/etc/apache2$ sudo vi /etc/apache2/ports.conf
```

```
Listen 80
Listen 8880
```

In addition, add port 8880 to your firewall.

```
vishne0@ubuntu:/$ sudo ufw allow 8880/tcp
Rules updated
Rules updated (v6)
```

To proceed you must now disable the default site.

```
vishne0@ubuntu:/etc/apache2$ sudo a2dissite 000-default
Site 000-default disabled.
```

Now, enable Graphite-web, as follows:

```
vishne0@ubuntu:/etc/apache2$ sudo a2ensite apache2-graphite
Enabling site apache2-graphite.
```

To activate the new configuration, you have to run `service apache2 reload`. Restart Apache to invoke the changes.

```
vishne0@ubuntu:/etc/apache2$ sudo service apache2 reload
```

Let's check if Apache is running.

```
vishne0@ubuntu:/etc/apache2$ sudo service apache2 status
apache2.service - LSB: Apache2 web server
   Loaded: loaded (/etc/init.d/apache2; bad; vendor preset: enabled)
  Drop-In: /lib/systemd/system/apache2.service.d
           └─apache2-systemd.conf
   Active: active (running) since Mon 2016-10-10 14:21:40 UTC; 35min ago
     Docs: man:systemd-sysv-generator(8)
  Process: 12885 ExecReload=/etc/init.d/apache2 reload (code=exited, status=0/SUCCESS)
   CGroup: /system.slice/apache2.service
           ├──11880 /usr/sbin/apache2 -k start
           ├──12908 /usr/sbin/apache2 -k start
           ├──12909 (wsgi:_graphite)  -k start
           ├──12910 (wsgi:_graphite)  -k start
           ├──12911 (wsgi:_graphite)  -k start
           ├──12912 (wsgi:_graphite)  -k start
           ├──12913 (wsgi:_graphite)  -k start
           ├──12914 Passenger watchdog
           ├──12917 Passenger core
           ├──12922 Passenger ust-router
           ├──12933 /usr/sbin/apache2 -k start
           └──12934 /usr/sbin/apache2 -k start
Oct 10 14:21:39 ubuntu systemd[1]: Starting LSB: Apache2 web server...
Oct 10 14:21:39 ubuntu apache2[11840]:  * Starting Apache httpd web server apache2
Oct 10 14:21:39 ubuntu apache2[11840]: AH00112: Warning: DocumentRoot [/usr/share/foreman/
public] does not exist
Oct 10 14:21:39 ubuntu apache2[11840]: AH00112: Warning: DocumentRoot [/usr/share/foreman/
public] does not exist
Oct 10 14:21:40 ubuntu apache2[11840]:  *
Oct 10 14:21:40 ubuntu systemd[1]: Started LSB: Apache2 web server.
Oct 10 14:56:35 ubuntu systemd[1]: Reloading LSB: Apache2 web server.
Oct 10 14:56:35 ubuntu apache2[12885]:  * Reloading Apache httpd web server apache2
Oct 10 14:56:36 ubuntu apache2[12885]:  *
Oct 10 14:56:36 ubuntu systemd[1]: Reloaded LSB: Apache2 web server.
```

Database Creation

It's time to create the database, as we are using the default setup.

```
vishneo@ubuntu:/etc/apache2$ cd /usr/lib/python2.7/dist-packages/graphite/
vishneo@ubuntu:/usr/lib/python2.7/dist-packages/graphite$ sudo python manage.py syncdb
```

It will ask you to create a superuser, so say Yes. Then it will ask you few questions, so just follow the process.

```
vishneo@ubuntu:/usr/lib/python2.7/dist-packages/graphite$ sudo python manage.py syncdb
You have installed Django's auth system, and don't have any superusers defined.
Would you like to create one now? (yes/no): yes
```

Once you've finished, the database is created.

```
vishneo@ubuntu:/$ sudo chown _graphite:_graphite /var/lib/graphite/graphite.db
```

Check to see if Graphite is running on your server at port 8880 (Figure 6-15). Point your browser to http://yourip:8880.

Figure 6-15. *Graphite is running on Ubuntu 16.04.1 LTS*

Check to see if any data is coming up (Figure 6-16).

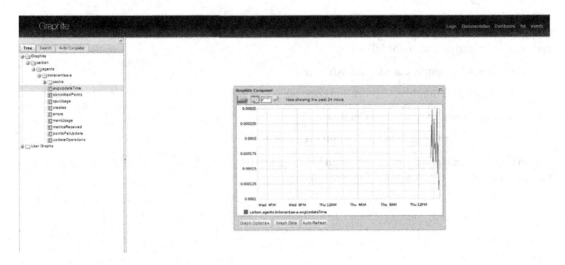

Figure 6-16. *Graphite showing data*

Configuring Logstash to Send Output to Graphite

As you have done in earlier sections, you will use the 06-graphitemetrics.conf file here as well.

```
vishne0@ubuntu:/$:/etc/logstash/conf.d$ sudo vi 06-graphitemetrics.conf
```

Copy the content of the conf file in this one, and restart Logstash and Carbon. Change the path of the Apache log file to /var/log/apache2/access.log.
Test the config first, as follows:

```
vishne0@ubuntu:/etc/logstash/conf.d$ sudo service logstash configtest
If you see Configuration OK all is ok to go ahead
vishne0@ubuntu:/etc/logstash/conf.d$ sudo service logstash restart
vishne0@ubuntu:/etc/logstash/conf.d$ sudo service carbon-cache restart
```

Apache log files are owned by root, and Logstash user doesn't have the required permissions to read them. Thus, to read the file, you have to grant these permissions to Logstash user, as follows:

```
vishne0@ubuntu:/$ sudo setfacl -m u:logstash:r /var/log/apache2/access.log
```

It should now be working as it had on CentOS 7.

Summary

In this chapter, you installed Graphite on CentOS 7 and Ubuntu 16.04.1 LTS and configured Logstash to send output to Graphite using Logstash graphite. You have also learned what the Logstash and Graphite setups can be used for and how to do the following:

- Install Graphite, Carbon, and Whisper

- Configure Graphite, Carbon, and Logstash

- Configure Apache to run Graphite-web

- Configure Logstash to send output to Graphite

In next chapter, you will learn more about how to get alerts and notifications, based on changes in data, using Watcher, which is a plug-in for Elasticsearch.

CHAPTER 7

■ ■ ■

Configuring Elasticsearch Watcher

In the previous chapter, you configured Graphite with Logstash to access time-based data and graphs to compare results. It's also a good configuration for server admins to use to view and analyze the performance of services and applications.

Over the last few years, however, server admins had to work toward making servers and applications more secure. To accomplish this, they often looked for new ways to receive notifications or alerts. Configuring the ELK Stack makes server admins' lives a lot easier, because they can monitor logs from different servers at a centralized location and analyze them as well.

However, if more information is required, you'll want to trace the incidents on your servers. You'll want to have notifications and alerts sent to you for any suspicious activity. In addition, you may also want to see notifications and alerts about the health of your server, server load, storage space left on the device, and so forth. To achieve this, an excellent plug-in for Elasticsearch is available: Elasticsearch Watcher. With the Watcher API, you can create, manage, and check your "watches."

Watcher is a commercial product, and you can get a 30-day trial license. It's recommended that you use it on your production servers, to implement a proper alerting system.

We will now install and configure Watcher.

Installing Watcher on CentOS 7

As you have already installed Elasticsearch on the server, you only have to install the plug-in now. By default, the Elasticsearch installation directory is /usr/share/elasticsearch/. Let's change the directory.

```
[vishne0@centylog /]$ cd /usr/share/elasticsearch/
```

Next, you will install the license and plug-in.

```
[vishne0@centylog elasticsearch]$ sudo bin/plugin install license
-> Installing license...
Trying https://download.elastic.co/elasticsearch/release/org/elasticsearch/plugin/
license/2.4.0/license-2.4.0.zip ...
Downloading .......DONE
Verifying https://download.elastic.co/elasticsearch/release/org/elasticsearch/plugin/
license/2.4.0/license-2.4.0.zip checksums if available ...
Downloading .DONE
```

The license is now installed. Next, let's install the Watcher plug-in.

```
[vishne0@centylog elasticsearch]$ sudo bin/plugin install watcher
-> Installing watcher...
Trying https://download.elastic.co/elasticsearch/release/org/elasticsearch/plugin/
watcher/2.4.0/watcher-2.4.0.zip ...
Downloading ...............................................................................
................DONE
Verifying https://download.elastic.co/elasticsearch/release/org/elasticsearch/plugin/
watcher/2.4.0/watcher-2.4.0.zip checksums if available ...
Downloading. DONE
@@@@@@@@@@@@@@@@@@@@@@@@@@@@@@@@@@@@@@@@@@@@@@@@@@@@@@@@@@@@@@@
@     WARNING: plugin requires additional permissions      @
@@@@@@@@@@@@@@@@@@@@@@@@@@@@@@@@@@@@@@@@@@@@@@@@@@@@@@@@@@@@@@@
* java.lang.RuntimePermission getClassLoader
* java.lang.RuntimePermission setContextClassLoader
* java.lang.RuntimePermission setFactory
See http://docs.oracle.com/javase/8/docs/technotes/guides/security/permissions.html
for descriptions of what these permissions allow and the associated risks.
```

You must answer "yes" to the preceding warning, as the Watcher plug-in requires these permissions in order to work properly.

```
Continue with installation? [y/N]y
Installed watcher into /usr/share/elasticsearch/plugins/watcher
```

The Watcher plug-in is now installed on your server. Restart Elasticsearch.

```
[vishne0@centylog elasticsearch]$ sudo service elasticsearch restart
```

To test if Watcher is working, run the following commands:

```
[vishne0@centylog elasticsearch]$ curl -XGET 'http://localhost:9200/_watcher/stats?pretty'
{
  "watcher_state" : "started",
  "watch_count" : 0,
  "execution_thread_pool" : {
    "queue_size" : 0,
    "max_size" : 0
  },
  "manually_stopped" : false
}
```

As shown in Figure 7-1, the plug-in is working and showing you the output as well. Let's view the output.

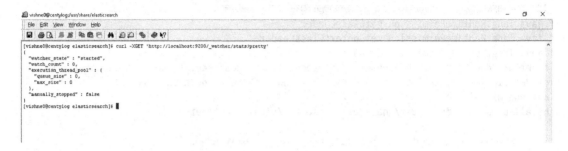

Figure 7-1. *Testing Watcher installation*

There are two things on which you need to focus: watch_count and execution_thread_pool. watch_count has a value of 0, and execution_thread_pool is empty, because we didn't set up any watches yet, but that's OK.

Remember: The trial version of Watcher is valid for 30 days, and you can use all the features. After 30 days, you must buy a subscription in order to use it.

Installing Watcher on Ubuntu 16.04.1 LTS

Installing Watcher on an Ubuntu 16.04.1 LTS machine is similar to installing Watcher on CentOS 7. You have to run the following commands:

```
vishne0@Ubuntu:~# cd /usr/share/elasticsearch/
vishne0@Ubuntu:~# /usr/share/elasticsearch$ sudo bin/plugin install license
-> Installing license...
Trying https://download.elastic.co/elasticsearch/release/org/elasticsearch/plugin/
license/2.4.0/license-2.4.0.zip ...
Downloading .......DONE
Verifying https://download.elastic.co/elasticsearch/release/org/elasticsearch/plugin/
license/2.4.0 /license-2.4.0.zip checksums if available ...
Downloading .DONE
Installed license into /usr/share/elasticsearch/plugins/license
Installing Watcher plugin:
vishne0@Ubuntu:~ # /usr/share/elasticsearch$ sudo bin/plugin install watcher
-> Installing watcher...
Trying https://download.elastic.co/elasticsearch/release/org/elasticsearch/plugin/
watcher/2.4.0/watcher-2.4.0.zip ...
Downloading ...................................................................
................DONE
Verifying https://download.elastic.co/elasticsearch/release/org/elasticsearch/plugin/
watcher/2.4.0/watcher-2.4.0.zip checksums if available ...
Downloading .DONE
```

```
@@@@@@@@@@@@@@@@@@@@@@@@@@@@@@@@@@@@@@@@@@@@@@@@@@@@@@@@@@@@@@@
@     WARNING: plugin requires additional permissions     @
@@@@@@@@@@@@@@@@@@@@@@@@@@@@@@@@@@@@@@@@@@@@@@@@@@@@@@@@@@@@@@@
* java.lang.RuntimePermission getClassLoader
* java.lang.RuntimePermission setContextClassLoader
* java.lang.RuntimePermission setFactory
See http://docs.oracle.com/javase/8/docs/technotes/guides/security/permissions.html
for descriptions of what these permissions allow and the associated risks.
Continue with installation? [y/N]y
Installed watcher into /usr/share/elasticsearch/plugins/watcher
```

Watcher is now installed. Next, restart Elasticsearch and test Watcher.

```
vishne0@Ubuntu:~# /usr/share/elasticsearch$ sudo service elasticsearch restart
```

To test whether Watcher is working, run the following commands:

```
vishne0@Ubuntu:~# curl -XGET 'http://localhost:9200/_watcher/stats?pretty'
{
  "watcher_state" : "started",
  "watch_count" : 0,
  "execution_thread_pool" : {
    "queue_size" : 0,
    "max_size" : 0
  },
  "manually_stopped" : false
}
```

Watcher is installed properly on our Ubuntu 16.04.1 LTS server. As explained previously, the watch_count has a value of 0, and execution_thread_pool is empty, as you haven't configured any watches yet.

Configuring Watches for Logs

Configuring a watch to check logs in a given time period is easy. The main components that you should have in your watch are scheduling, condition, and action. Scheduling is important for checking logs periodically for events. Condition is added to see if there are any alerts. If your watch finds an alert, you should have defined an action to be taken, such as sending an e-mail, and so forth.

Let's configure a watch using these three components. In Chapter 1, we created an index named Logstash. Let's use that index in our watch. The following watch will search the Logstash index for errors every 15 seconds. Use curl to call the Watcher API.

```
[vishne0@centylog]$curl -XPUT 'http://localhost:9200/_watcher/watch/logstash_watch' -d '{
  "trigger" : {
    "schedule" : { "interval" : "15s" }
  },
  "input" : {
    "search" : {
      "request" : {
        "indices" : [ "logstash" ],
        "body" : {
```

```
          "query" : {
            "match" : { "message": "error" }
          }
        }
      }
    }
  }
},
"condition" : {
    "compare" : { "ctx.payload.hits.total" : { "gt" : 0 }}
  }
},
"actions" : {
    "log_error" : {
      "logging" : {
        "text" : "Found {{ctx.payload.hits.total}} errors in the logs"
      }
    }
  }
}'
```

When you run this code, it should produce the following message:

```
{"_id":"logstash_watch","_version":1,"created":true}
```

This means that your watch is created and running. Now let's see what the preceding code is actually doing.

- You can schedule a control to check how often a watch should be triggered. The
  code "schedule" : {"interval" : "15s"}" is a trigger that will execute every 15
  seconds. The input will get the data to evaluate and use search, so that a watch can
  search for the data in your logs.

- You have added a condition to see if any error is found in the logs. The code
  "condition" : {"compare" : {"ctx.payload.hits.total" : {"gt" : 0 }}} is
  added to check it. The parameter compare lets us compare the values.

- Another important step is to add an action. You have configured a watch to make
  sure that you receive alerts or notifications of events. The parameter "actions"
  defines what action is needed once the condition is met. You can send an
  e-mail or write the error into a file. The code "actions" : {   "log_error" :
  {   "logging" : {   "text" : "Found {{ctx.payload.hits.total}}
  errors in the logs" is sending the message to Elasticsearch whenever it finds an
  error.

To check it, let's run another command that was run in an earlier section:

```
[vishne0@centylog]$ curl -XGET 'http://localhost:9200/_watcher/stats?pretty'
        And the output is:
        {
  "watcher_state" : "started",
  "watch_count" : 1,
  "execution_thread_pool" : {
    "queue_size" : 0,
```

```
    "max_size" : 5
  },
  "manually_stopped" : false
}
```

As you can see clearly, the watch_count is now 1, which means that the watch has been created and will be monitoring the Logstash index every 15 seconds. All three conditions are included in the preceding code. You will see more examples in upcoming sections, which will help you understand more about defining actions when an error is detected.

Now delete the watch that you've created that checks the index every 15 seconds, as we will do a more realistic configuration next, and it will create more issues. To delete a watch, issue the following command:

```
[vishne0@centylog]$ curl -XDELETE 'http://localhost:9200/_watcher/watch/logstash_watch'
```

This will delete the watch that you had created for our experiment.

Configuring Kibana for Watches

In the previous section, you learned how to create and delete watches in Elasticsearch. You will now see how we can integrate the watches with Kibana. Let's use the same example as in the previous section, to create a watch to monitor the errors in the logs.

```
[vishne0@centylog /]$ curl -XPUT 'http://localhost:9200/_watcher/watch/logstash_watch' -d '{
  "trigger" : {
    "schedule" : { "interval" : "15s" }
  },
  "input" : {
    "search" : {
      "request" : {
        "indices" : [ "logstash" ],
        "body" : {
          "query" : {
            "match" : { "message": "error" }
          }
        }
      }
    }
  }
},
"condition" : {
    "compare" : { "ctx.payload.hits.total" : { "gt" : 0 }}
  }
},
"actions" : {
    "log_error" : {
      "logging" : {
        "text" : "Found {{ctx.payload.hits.total}} errors in the logs"
      }
    }
  }
}'
```

Watcher maintains a full history of all watches, and a new history index is created daily with .watch_history-YYYY-MM.DD. Search for the index with .watch_history*.

Once you run the preceding code, open a browser and point it to http://yourip:5601. Then open Kibana, go to settings, and in the index name or pattern field, type .watch_history*. In the Time-field name, select trigger_event.triggered_time. You will see a screen similar to the one shown in Figure 7-2.

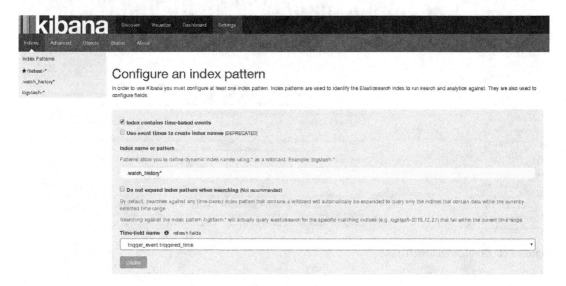

Figure 7-2. *Creating an index pattern for watches in Kibana*

As you can see in Figure 7-2, click the Create button, and it's done. Click the Discover tab at the top left of the screen, select the newly created Index Pattern, .watch_history*, and you will see a screen similar to the one shown in Figure 7-3.

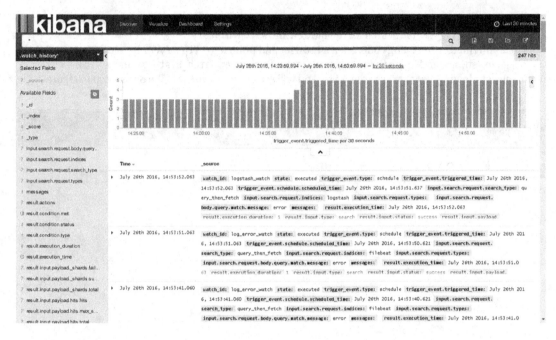

Figure 7-3. *Configured watch data*

Figure 7-3 shows us the result of all the configured watches on the system.

Sending Alerts to E-mail

You can configure Watcher to send alerts to an e-mail ID. Here, I am going to talk about configuring a Gmail account only. In your Watcher JSON, you have to add the following code:

```
"actions": {
        "email_admin": {
            "email": {
                "to": "'Admin <vishne0@gmail.com >'",
                "subject": "{{ctx.watch_id}} executed",
                "body": "{{ctx.watch_id}} executed with {{ctx.payload.hits.total}} hits"
            }
        }
    }
}
```

Now you have to add the following code to `elasticsearch.yml`. Add it to the end of the file.

```
watcher.actions.email.service.account:
    work:
        profile: gmail
        email_defaults:
            from: 'Admin <admin@host.domain>'
            bcc: supprt@host.domain
```

```
smtp:
    auth: true
    starttls.enable: true
    host: smtp.gmail.com
    port: 587
    user: <username>
    password: <password>
```

That's it. Now you can receive notifications in your Gmail account.

Configuring Sense Editor

Thus far, you have been creating watches using the command line. Though it's OK to create watches from the command line, it would be better if you had an editor to write your code and run it simultaneously. To achieve this, install Sense Editor, with which you can type and submit requests to Elasticsearch and also run it using the Sense Editor console.

Installing Sense Editor

Sense Editor is a Kibana app. As you already have Kibana installed, all you have to do is to go to the bin directory of Kibana and install the plug-in. The installation process is the same both for CentOS 7 and Ubuntu 16.04.1 LTS.

```
[vishne0@centylog /]$ cd /opt/kibana/
[vishne0@centylog kibana]$ sudo ./bin/kibana plugin --install elastic/sense
```

As shown in Figure 7-4, the Sense Editor is installed properly.

Figure 7-4. *Installing the Sense Editor for Kibana*

To open the Sense Editor, open a browser and point it to http://yourip:5601/app/sense. You will be greeted with a screen similar to that shown in Figure 7-5.

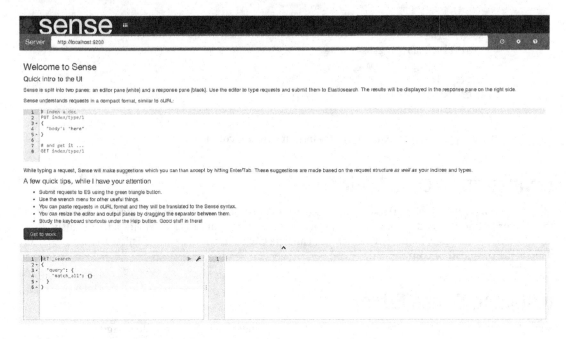

Figure 7-5. Sense Editor opening screen

Next, click the Get to work button, and you will see a screen similar to that shown in Figure 7-6.

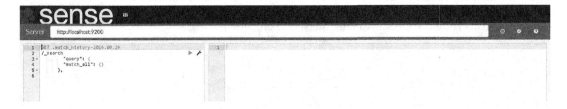

Figure 7-6. Sense Editor showing two panes

As you can see in Figure 7-6, the Sense Editor shows two panes. The pane on the left is the editor in which you will enter your code to submit to Elasticsearch and to create the watches. The right pane displays the responses from Elasticsearch. In previous sections, you have submitted your code to Elasticsearch from the command line. Next, you will submit your code to Elasticsearch using Sense app, and you will see the response as well.

Here, I have written the code to search the .watch_history index with the date:

```
GET .watch_history-2016.09.29
/_search
        "query": {
        "match_all": {}
    },
```

Just click the green button next to _search on the right side. Once you click the button, you will see the following response from Elasticsearch. As you can see in Figure 7-7, Elasticsearch shows the response to the code you have written in Sense. The output pane is showing us the result of the .watch_history-YYYY-MM-DD search.

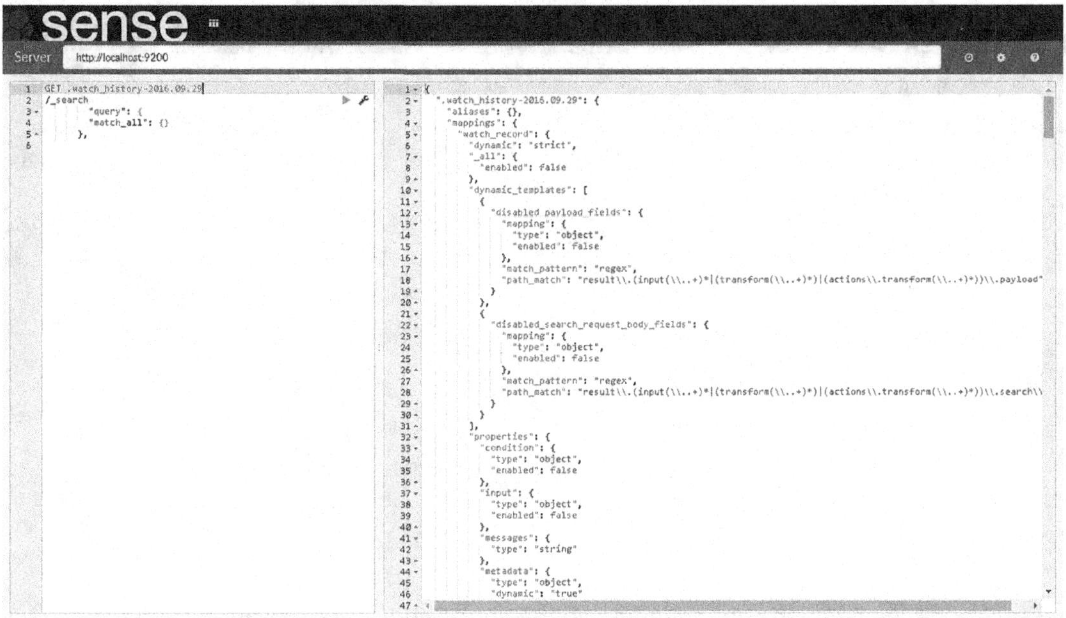

Figure 7-7. *The reponse from Elasticsearch*

You can write watches in the Sense Editor and see the response as well. Sense takes the commands in curl-like syntax, as we ran the watches code using the Linux command line.

Creating an Index Using Sense

You can easily create an index using Sense. For example, see the following:

```
PUT /apache_error?pretty=true
{
  "acknowledged": true
}
```

When you run this code from the Sense Editor, Elasticsearch will create an index.

Listing Watches

You can list all of your watches stored in `.watches index`. Using Sense Editor, you can search all the configured watches (Figure 7-8).

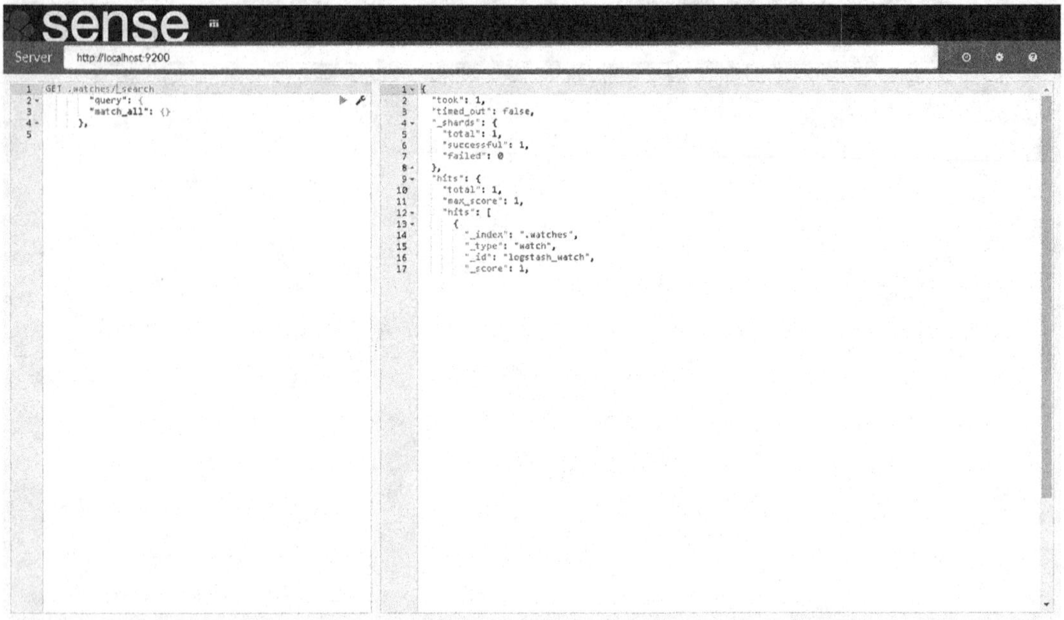

Figure 7-8. *A search for configured watches*

As you can see in Figure 7-8, the watches that you have configured are shown. Thus far, only watch is configured.

Deleting Watches

You can delete watches permanently, using Sense or from the command line, as follows:

```
[vishne0@centylog /]$curl -XDELETE 'http://localhost:9200/_watcher/watch/logstash_watch'
 From Sense
DELETE _watcher/watch/logstash_watch
```

Sense Editor History

You can check history with the Sense Editor UI, by clicking the Clock button next to the server field in the upper-right corner of the screen. Once you click the Clock button, we will see a screen similar to that shown in Figure 7-9.

Figure 7-9. *Sense Editor history*

Sense can show as many as the last 500 requests made to Elasticsearch.

Sense Editor Settings

Next to history, you will see a Settings button. From there, you can check and apply the Settings options provided by Sense. Once you click the Settings button, you will see a screen similar to that shown in Figure 7-10.

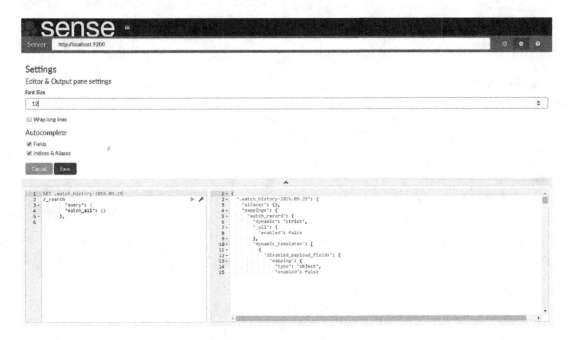

Figure 7-10. *Settings section of the Sense UI*

The Settings screen provides a few options. They are:

- *Font Size*: You can adjust font size with this option.

- *Wrap long lines*: Use this to wrap long outputs.

- *Autocomplete*: This is an interesting option, and you should enable both the Fields and Indexes and the Aliases options. When you write your code in Sense Editor, autocomplete helps to see which Fields are there. Autocomplete for Indexes and Aliases helps you to quickly select the correct ones, as many might be saved.

Sense Editor Help

Help appears next to the Settings button. Click it, and you will see a screen similar to that shown in Figure 7-11. There are two tabs on this screen:

- *Request format*: This shows how you can write the code in Sense Editor.

- *Keyboard tips*: These are keys that you can use in the editor.

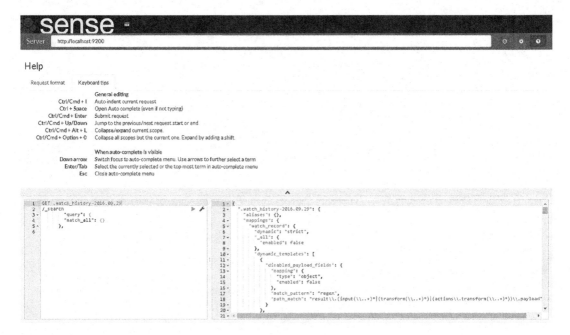

Figure 7-11. *Sense Editor Help screen*

Summary

In this chapter, you installed the Watcher and Sense Editor plug-ins on CentOS 7 and Ubuntu 16.04.1 TLS. You successfully configured Watcher, and you were able to see the output using Kibana. You also installed a Kibana app called Sense Editor, to run inside Kibana and to send code inputs to Elasticsearch. You also learned about Sense UI and how to do following:

- Check history in the Sense UI

- Adjust Settings in the Sense UI

- View the Help section in the Sense UI

In next chapter, you will learn how to secure a cluster, using the Shield plug-in for Elasticsearch. I will be covering the following topics:

- How to prevent unauthorized access

- How to protect the integrity of the data

- How to audit your data

■ ■ ■

## CHAPTER 8

Securing the ELK Stack with Shield

By now you have ELK Stack configured and running. Nevertheless, we still haven't addressed the most important part: security. When you deploy ELK Stack to a production environment, you cannot let the world have access to your data. You need a system and a set of restrictions for accessing your data. Today, when hackers, script kiddies, and bots are scouring the Internet for private corporate information, you must make sure that your data is secure and know just who is accessing that data and what they are retrieving.

Shield is a plug-in for Elasticsearch, and it is what you need to secure your Elasticsearch clusters. In a nutshell, here are the main Shield features:

- IP filtering

- Authentication

- Authorization

- Node encryption

- Auditing

To learn more about these features, let's install the Shield plug-in for Elasticsearch. Shield is a commercial plug-in, and a 30-day free-trial license is available.

Elastic Shield is a commercial plug-in. You will have to pay for it once the trial period expires. Why am I recommending a commercial product here? The answer is that when speaking about production servers and ELK clusters, you'll require a program that has 24/7 support. If something goes wrong, you will be able to call someone to resolve the issue, rather than searching through public forums and possibly waiting for an answer to your question. Downtime in a production environment is very expensive for a company. Furthermore, the commercial plug-in is always up to date, with the latest versions of ELK Stack. To obtain a commercial license, you can subscribe using the following link: `www.elastic.co/subscriptions`.

Search Guard is an open source alternative to Shield. It is available at the following address: `https://floragunn.com/searchguard/`.

Preinstallation Setup

To install the latest version of Shield, you should have the following:

- Java 7 or Java 8

- Elasticsearch 2.4 and the Elasticsearch license

© Vishal Sharma 2016

V. Sharma, *Beginning Elastic Stack*, DOI 10.1007/978-1-4842-1694-1_8

Installing Shield on CentOS 7

On CentOS 7, the Elasticsearch home directory is set at /usr/share/elasticsearch. To change the directory, use the following:

```
[vishne0@centylog ~]$ cd /usr/share/elasticsearch/
```

Once inside the directory, you will install the plug-in.

```
[vishne0@centylog elasticsearch sudo bin/plugin install shield
[sudo] password for vishne0:
-> Installing shield...
Trying https://download.elastic.co/elasticsearch/release/org/elasticsearch/plugin/
shield/2.4.0/shield-2.4.0.zip ...
Downloading .....................................................................
...........................................................DONE
Verifying https://download.elastic.co/elasticsearch/release/org/elasticsearch/plugin/
shield/2.4.0/shield-2.4.0.zip checksums if available ...
Downloading .DONE
@@@@@@@@@@@@@@@@@@@@@@@@@@@@@@@@@@@@@@@@@@@@@@@@@@@@@@@@@@@@@@@@
@     WARNING: plugin requires additional permissions     @
@@@@@@@@@@@@@@@@@@@@@@@@@@@@@@@@@@@@@@@@@@@@@@@@@@@@@@@@@@@@@@@@
* java.lang.RuntimePermission setFactory
```

Visit the following link for descriptions of what these permissions allow and their associated risks: http://docs.oracle.com/javase/8/docs/technotes/guides/security/permissions.html.

```
Continue with installation? [y/N]y
Installed shield into /usr/share/elasticsearch/plugins/shield
```

Now that Shield is installed, as seen in Figure 8-1, let's start Elasticsearch:

```
[vishne0@centylog ~]$ sudo service elasticsearch start
```

```
[vishne0@centylog elasticsearch]$ sudo bin/plugin install shield
[sudo] password for vishne0:
-> Installing shield...
Trying https://download.elastic.co/elasticsearch/release/org/elasticsearch/plugin/shield/2.4.0/shield-2.4.0.zip ...
Downloading .......................................................................................................................DONE
Verifying https://download.elastic.co/elasticsearch/release/org/elasticsearch/plugin/shield/2.4.0/shield-2.4.0.zip checksums if available ...
Downloading .DONE
@@@@@@@@@@@@@@@@@@@@@@@@@@@@@@@@@@@@@@@@@@@@@@@@@@@@@@@@@@@@
@     WARNING: plugin requires additional permissions     @
@@@@@@@@@@@@@@@@@@@@@@@@@@@@@@@@@@@@@@@@@@@@@@@@@@@@@@@@@@@@
* java.lang.RuntimePermission setFactory
See http://docs.oracle.com/javase/8/docs/technotes/guides/security/permissions.html
for descriptions of what these permissions allow and the associated risks.

Continue with installation? [y/N]y
Installed shield into /usr/share/elasticsearch/plugins/shield
[vishne0@centylog elasticsearch]$ █
```

Figure 8-1. *Installing Shield for Elasticsearch on CentOS 7*

This command checks the logs in /var/log/elasticsearch/youcluster.log, and you should see something like the following:

```
[2016-08-15 04:59:11,430][INFO ][plugins                    ] [centylog] modules [reindex,
lang-expression, lang-groovy], plugins [license, shield], sites []
```

Shield is now installed and loaded properly. You have to configure Shield for user authentication, but we will do that later.

Installing Shield on Ubuntu 16.04.1 LTS

The Ubuntu Elasticsearch home directory is located at /usr/share/elasticsearch. Change that directory to the following:

```
vishal_gnutech@instance-1:/$ cd /usr/share/elasticsearch/
```

Now we will install Shield for Elasticsearch. First, install the license.

```
vishal_gnutech@instance-1:/usr/share/elasticsearch$ sudo bin/plugin install license
```

Now let's install the plug-in.

```
vishal_gnutech@instance-1:/usr/share/elasticsearch$ sudo bin/plugin install shield
```

Shield is now installed on Ubuntu 16.04.1 LTS, as shown in Figure 8-2. Restart Elasticsearch to load the plugin.

```
Vishal_gnutech@instance-1:sudo service elasticsearch restart
```

Figure 8-2. *Installing Shield for Elasticsearch on Ubuntu 16.04.1*

As you can see in Figure 8-3, Shield is loaded and displaying a message that your plug-in is running, but it didn't find any user in file /etc/elasticsearch/shield/users. We will configure the user in a later section. Before we move ahead, let's review some Shield features in depth.

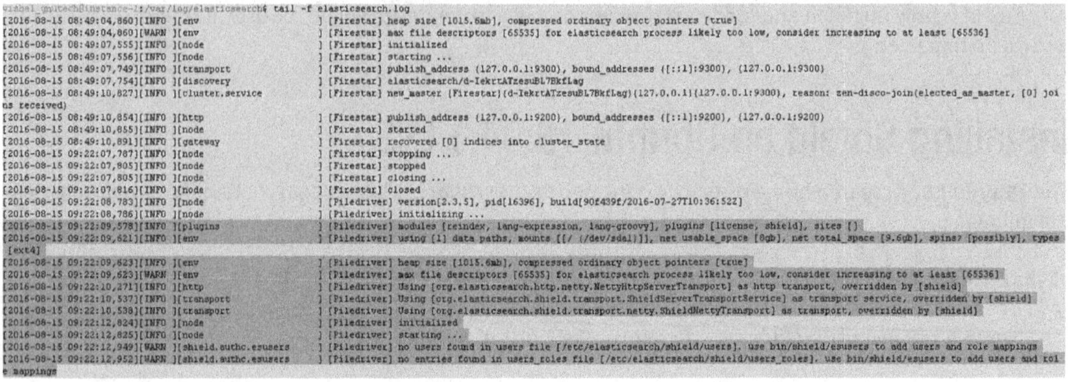

Figure 8-3. *Shield for Elasticsearch is loaded*

IP Filtering

You can do application-level filtering of IP addresses and decide what IPs you wish to allow and disallow. For example, you can write a rule such as the following in your `elasticsearch.yml`. To allow an IP:

```
shield.transport.filter.allow: "192.168.1.1"
```

To disallow an IP:

```
shield.transport.filter.deny: "192.168.1.10"
```

One thing to note here is that allow rules will always appear first, followed by deny rules. For example, they should be arranged as follows:

```
shield.transport.filter.allow: "192.168.1.1"
shield.transport.filter.deny: "192.168.1.10"
```

These are just examples for now; you will see more realistic approaches in later sections. Similarly, you can allow multiple IPs.

```
shield.transport.filter.allow: ["192.168.1.1", "192.168.1.11",
"192.168.1.21", 192.168.1.99"]
```

You can use an array as well, which will block all connections that are not allowed.

```
shield.transport.filter.deny: _all
```

You can do hostname filtering by using the following statement:

```
shield.transport.filter.deny: '*.yahoo.com'
```

Authentication

Shield provides various methods for authentication. *Authentication* means that users must prove their identity, either by passwords, keys, or anything else that you want to check as input.

Shield supports various methods to authenticate a user. Per the official Shield documents, a realm is used to authenticate users. A realm is a user database employed by the Shield plug-in. The following types of realms are supported by Shield:

- *Native*: This is the default built-in authentication system of Shield. You can add users, remove users, or assign roles using the REST API. For more information on how the REST API works, visit www.elastic.co/guide/en/shield/current/native-realm.html.

- *File*: As the name suggests, this is a file-based authentication system built into Shield by default.

Shield also supports external systems to authenticate users:

- *LDAP*: Authentication using the LDAP protocol.

- *Active Directory*: Authentication using the Active Directory protocol.

- *PKI*: Authentication via a public key

Adding a User to Shield

Now let's start with adding an admin user.

```
[vishne0@centylog elasticsearch]$ sudo bin/shield/esusers useradd es_admin -r admin -p admin123
```

Now when we add a user in Shield, it updates two files in /etc/elasticsearch/shield: users and users_role. There is another file, roles.yml, in which you can see the roles defined by default, as follows (see also Figure 8-4):

```
[vishne0@centylog /]$# sudo vi /etc/elasticsearch/shield/roles.yml
# All cluster rights
# All operations on all indices
admin:
  cluster:
    - all
  indices:
    - names: '*'
      privileges:
        - all

# monitoring cluster privileges
# All operations on all indices
power_user:
  cluster:
    - monitor
  indices:
    - names: '*'
      privileges:
        - all
```

```
# Read-only operations on indices
user:
  indices:
    - names: '*'
      privileges:
        - read

# Defines the required permissions for transport clients
transport_client:
  cluster:
      - transport_client

# The required permissions for the kibana 4 server
kibana4_server:
  cluster:
      - monitor
  indices:
    - names: '.kibana'
      privileges:
        - all
```

```
  All cluster rights
# All operations on all indices
admin:
  cluster:
    - all
  indices:
    - names: '*'
      privileges:
        - all

# monitoring cluster privileges
# All operations on all indices
power_user:
  cluster:
    - monitor
  indices:
    - names: '*'
      privileges:
        - all

# Read-only operations on indices
user:
  indices:
    - names: '*'
      privileges:
        - read

# Defines the required permissions for transport clients
transport_client:
  cluster:
      - transport_client

# The required permissions for the kibana 4 server
kibana4_server:
  cluster:
      - monitor
  indices:
    - names: '.kibana'
      privileges:
        - all
"/etc/elasticsearch/shield/roles.yml" 69L, 1355C
```

Figure 8-4. *The content of* `roles.yml`

Save and quit the editor by entering :wq and pressing Enter. Now that you have added a user, restart Elasticsearch, as follows:

```
[vishne0@centylog elasticsearch]$ sudo service elasticsearch restart
```

Let's check to see if we can connect to Elasticsearch without a user.

```
[vishne0@centylog elasticsearch]$ curl -XGET 'http://localhost:9200/'
{"error":{"root_cause":[{"type":"security_exception","reason":"missing authentication token
for REST request [/]","header":{"WWW-Authenticate":"Basic realm=\"shield\""}}],"type":"secur
ity_exception","reason":"missing authentication token for REST request [/]","header":{"WWW-
Authenticate":"Basic realm=\"shield\""}},"status":401}
```

As you can see, we can't, so let's now access it using user admin, which we created earlier.

```
[vishne0@centylog elasticsearch]$ curl -u es_admin -XGET 'http://localhost:9200/'
Enter host password for user 'es_admin':
{
  "name" : "centylog",
  "cluster_name" : "Cluster 1",
  "version" : {
    "number" : "2.3.5",
    "build_hash" : "90f439ff60a3c0f497f91663701e64ccd01edbb4",
    "build_timestamp" : "2016-07-27T10:36:52Z",
    "build_snapshot" : false,
    "lucene_version" : "5.5.0"
  },
  "tagline" : "You Know, for Search"
}
```

Now the Elasticsearch data is secured with Shield, as shown in Figure 8-5.

```
[vishne0@centylog ~]$ curl -u es_admin -XGET 'http://localhost:9200/'
Enter host password for user 'es_admin':
{
  "name" : "Centylog",
  "cluster_name" : "Linode-centy",
  "version" : {
    "number" : "2.4.0",
    "build_hash" : "ce9f0c7394dee074091dd1bc4e9469251181fc55",
    "build_timestamp" : "2016-08-29T09:14:17Z",
    "build_snapshot" : false,
    "lucene_version" : "5.5.2"
  },
  "tagline" : "You Know, for Search"
}
```

Figure 8-5. *Testing user authentication*

Figure 8-6 shows you that you are getting an Authentication Exception. As you have added a user es_admin with admin privileges, you will first add it to Kibana, and then you will try to access the web interface. Change the directory to /opt/kibana/config and open kibana.yml. Go to the following section:

```
#elasticsearch.username:
# elasticsearch.password:
```

Uncomment both the fields and put the username/passwd as shown below
```
elasticsearch.username: "es_admin"
 elasticsearch.password: "admin123"
```

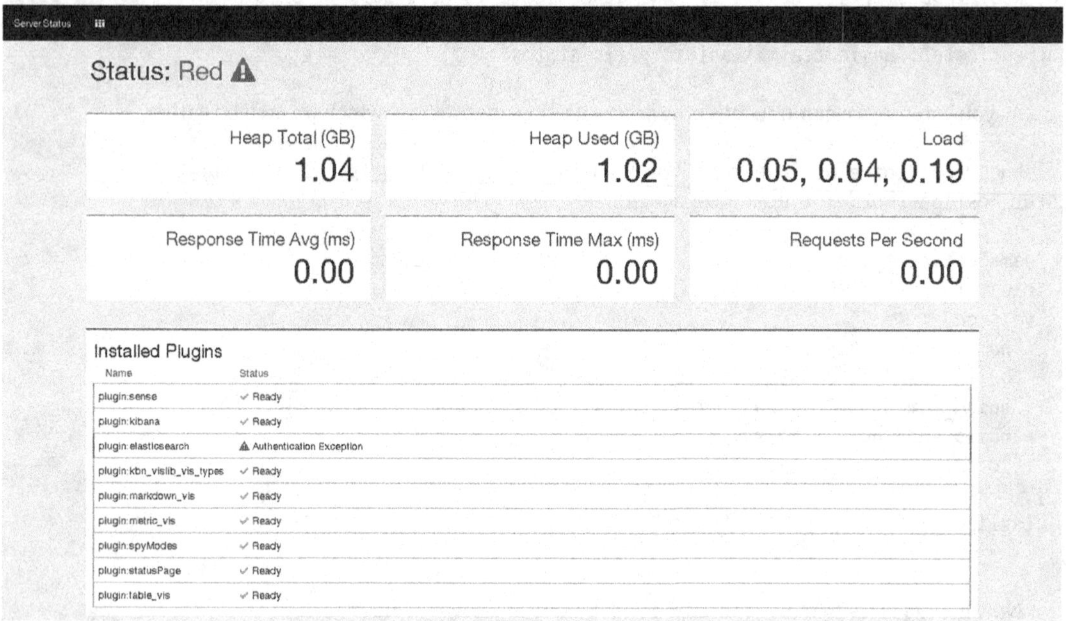

Figure 8-6. *Kibana can't access Elasticsearch data without user authentication*

We have enabled user authentication in Kibana, as shown in Figure 8-7. Now press :wq to write and quit from the vi editor. Restart Kibana.

```
[vishne0@centylog config]$ sudo service kibana restart
```

```
# The default application to load.
# kibana.defaultAppId: "discover"

# If your Elasticsearch is protected with basic auth, these are the user credentials
# used by the Kibana server to perform maintenance on the kibana_index at startup. Your Kibana
# users will still need to authenticate with Elasticsearch (which is proxied through
# the Kibana server)
 elasticsearch.username: "es_admin"
 elasticsearch.password: "admin123"
```

Figure 8-7. *Adding a user in kibana.yml*

We have enabled user authentication in Kibana, as shown in Figure 8-7. Now press :wq to write and quit from the vi editor. Restart Kibana.

```
[vishne0@centylog config]$ sudo service kibana restart
```

It's time to check if you can authenticate the Kibana interface with the credentials provided in kibana.yml. Open your browser and point it to http://localhost:5601 or, if it's running on a public IP, http://yourip:5601.

As you can see in Figure 8-8, Kibana is now asking for the authentication information. Use the information from kibana.yml, and you will be able to access the dashboard.

Figure 8-8. *Kibana is requesting authentication*

Configuring Logstash to Use Authentication

Now you have to make changes in the conf files that you created in your Logstash. All that you have to do is add the username and password in the output section of the config file and then restart Logstash. For example, in your 01-webserver.conf file, edit it and include the user/password fields, as shown here:

```
output {
  elasticsearch {
    hosts => ["localhost:9200"]
  user => es_admin
    password => admin123
  }
}
[vishne0@centylog conf.d]$ sudo service logstash restart
```

And that's all you really have to do to configure Logstash to use authentication.

Configuring Filebeat to Use Authentication

In Chapter 3, you installed Filebeat to send data from a remote server to your centralized ELK Stack. As you have now enabled authentication, you must make changes to Filebeat as well.

First, log into the remote server that you configured to send data to our ELK Stack, now for Filebeat. Once logged in, change the directory to /etc/filebeat and open filebeat.yml.

```
vishne0@srv [/etc/filebeat]# sudo vi filebeat.yml
```

Once the file is opened, go to the section ###Elasticsearch as output, and scroll down a bit until it says the following:

```
# Optional protocol and basic auth credentials.
    #protocol: "http"
    #username: "es_admin"
    #password: "password"
```

Now uncomment three lines—protocol, username, and password—and fill out the username and password that you have created. The protocol will be only "http". The final entries should look like the following:

```
protocol: "http"
    username: "es_admin"
    password: "admin123
```

In the password field, you will put the password that you have set. Press :wq to save the file and exit from the editor.

We have enabled authentication over http, as shown in Figure 8-9. Now let's check Kibana to see if we are receiving the data.

```
# Base config file used by all other beats for using libbeat features

############################# Output #########################################

# Configure what outputs to use when sending the data collected by the beat.
# Multiple outputs may be used.
output:

  ### Elasticsearch as output
  #elasticsearch:
    # Array of hosts to connect to.
    # Scheme and port can be left out and will be set to the default (http and 9200)
    # In case you specify and additional path, the scheme is required: http://localhost:9200/path
    # IPv6 addresses should always be defined as: https://[2001:db8::1]:9200
    # hosts: ["1 .1 .1 .2 :9200"]

    # Optional protocol and basic auth credentials.
    protocol: "https"
    username: "es_admin"
    password: "admin123"
```

Figure 8-9. *Configuring Filebeat to use authentication*

As you can see in Figure 8-10, Elasticsearch, Logstash, Kibana, and Filebeat are now using the authentication that you have configured, and your data now is secure.

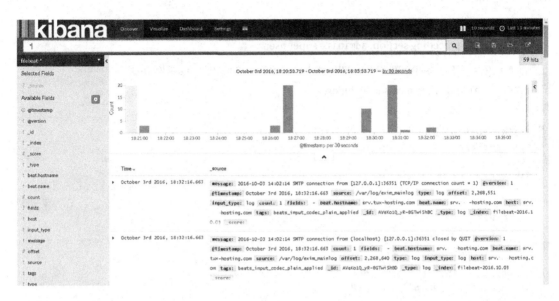

Figure 8-10. *Kibana displaying output from the remote server using Filebeat*

Authorization

While configuring the user, you have seen that `roles.yml` has predefined roles and authorization for Shield. Let's take a look at the `roles.yml` file.

```
[vishne0@centylog conf.d]$ sudo vi /etc/elasticsearch/shield/roles.yml
# All operations on all indices
admin:
  cluster:
    - all
  indices:
    - names: '*'
      privileges:
        - all

# monitoring cluster privileges
# All operations on all indices
power_user:
  cluster:
    - monitor
  indices:
    - names: '*'
      privileges:
        - all

# Read-only operations on indices
user:
  indices:
    - names: '*'
      privileges:
        - read
```

As you can see in Figure 8-11, user roles are defined.

- In the preceding section, admin is a super user.

- cluster is cluster-related privileges. Here, admins have privileges for all the clusters.

- - all provides access to all indexes.

```
# All cluster rights
# All operations on all indices
admin:
  cluster:
    - all
  indices:
    - names: '*'
      privileges:
        - all

# monitoring cluster privileges
# All operations on all indices
power_user:
  cluster:
    - monitor
  indices:
    - names: '*'
      privileges:
        - all

# Read-only operations on indices
user:
  indices:
    - names: '*'
      privileges:
        - read

# Defines the required permissions for transport clients
transport_client:
  cluster:
      - transport_client

# The required permissions for the kibana 4 server
kibana4_server:
  cluster:
      - monitor
 indices:
    - names: 'logstash-*'
      privileges:
        - view_index_metadata
        - read
"/etc/elasticsearch/shield/roles.yml" 74L, 1454C
```

Figure 8-11. *Showing the content of* roles.yml *in the Shield directory*

You can use predefined roles from this template while adding users with eusers. For example, you can add a user such as the following:

```
[vishne0@centylog elasticsearch]$ sudo bin/shield/esusers adduser -joe -p password -r logstash
```

Here, the user is inheriting the role of user Logstash.

```
# The required role for logstash users
logstash:
  cluster:
    - manage_index_templates
  indices:
    - names: 'logstash-*'
      privileges:
        - write
        - delete
        - create_index
```

Similarly, you can assign different roles and access privileges to different users.

Node Encryption

One of the features available in Shield is to encrypt traffic using SSL/TLS certificates. You can use a self-generated SSL/TLS certificate or a certificate authority (CA) signed by one of the certification authorities, such as Verisign. Traffic encryption halts the sniffing of your data in plain text. Refer to www.elastic.co/guide/en/shield/current/ssl-tls.html for more information.

Auditing of Security Events

It is very important that you keep track of events happening on your server, especially security events such as failed login attempts or perhaps refused connections or firewall warnings. Auditing gives you full insight into events on your nodes or information about attacks.

To enable auditing, all that you have to do is to add a line in your /etc/elasticsearch/elasticsearch.yml file.

```
shield.audit.enabled: true
```

You can save audit logs in two ways:

- In access.log
- By creating an Elasticsearch index on the same cluster

For outputs, you have to enable shield.audit.outputs: [index, logfile]. You can specify different log types, for example:

- authentication_failed [realm] for every realm failed authentication
- access_denied

...and a lot more. You can also specify such levels as WARN, DEBUG, ERROR, and so forth.

Audit logging settings must be configured in /etc/elasticsearch/shield/logging.yml.

[vishne0@centylog elasticsearch]$ sudo vi /etc/elasticsearch/shield/logging.yml

As you can see in Figure 8-12, by default, logs are stored in access.log, which is located in the /var/log/elasticsearch directory.

```
# default configuration for the audit trail logs
#
# Error Levels:
#
# ERROR   authentication_failed, access_denied, tampered_request, connection_denied
# WARN    authentication_failed, access_denied, tampered_request, connection_denied, anonymous_access
# INFO    authentication_failed, access_denied, tampered_request, connection_denied, anonymous_access, access_granted
# DEBUG   doesn't output additional entry types beyond INFO, but extends the information emitted for each entry
# TRACE   authentication_failed, access_denied, tampered_request, connection_denied, anonymous_access, access_granted, connection_granted, authentication_failed [<realm>]. In addition, intern
al system requests (self-management requests triggered by elasticsearch itself) will also be logged for "access_granted" entry type.
#

logger:
    shield.audit.logfile: INFO, access_log

additivity:
    shield.audit.logfile: false

appender:

    access_log:
      type: dailyRollingFile
      file: ${path.logs}/${cluster.name}-access.log
      datePattern: "'.'yyyy-MM-dd"
      layout:
        type: pattern
        conversionPattern: "[%d{ISO8601}] %m%n"
shield.audit.enabled: true
```

Figure 8-12. *Default* logging.yml

Summary

In this chapter, you learned how to secure your ELK Stack, using Shield and the basic authentication method. You also discovered some important Shield features, including

- IP filtering

- Authentication

- Authorization

- Node encryption

- Auditing

In the next chapter, you will learn about Logstash input and output plug-ins.

CHAPTER 9

■ ■ ■

Logstash Plug-ins

Logstash has many input plug-ins and codecs. All of the plug-ins are available as gems and hosted on rubygems.org. All of the plug-ins can be managed by bin/logstash-plugin. Using this script, you can install, uninstall, and remove plug-ins.

■ **Note** To learn more about gems, see: https://en.wikipedia.org/wiki/RubyGems.

To understand better how plug-ins work, take a look at the setup diagram shown in Figure 9-1.

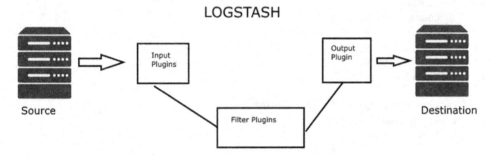

Figure 9-1. *How plug-ins work*

As you can see in Figure 9-1, when you receive data from the source, it has been processed by Input plug-ins first and then processed by Filter plug-ins, and, finally, an Output plug-in sends the data to destination as defined. For example, note the following configuration of file 01-webserver.conf, which you have created:

```
input {
file {
path => "/var/log/httpd/access_log"
start_position => "beginning"
}
}
```

In the preceding code snippet, input is defined as file and has provided the path. You will see more input options in later sections.

```
filter {
if [type] == "apache-access"
{
```

We are defining the filter solely to get the information needed from the log.

```
output {
elasticsearch {
hosts => ["localhost:9200"]
}
```

We have defined the output as elasticsearch. We will see more output options in later sections.

Let's see some examples using bin/logstash-plugin. First, to see what parameters are available, run the following command from /opt/logstash/:

```
[vishne0@centylog logstash]$ bin/logstash-plugin -h

Usage:
    bin/logstash-plugin [OPTIONS] SUBCOMMAND [ARG] ...
Parameters:
    SUBCOMMAND   subcommand
    [ARG] ...    subcommand arguments

Subcommands:
    install      Install a plugin
    uninstall    Uninstall a plugin
    update       Update a plugin
    pack         Package currently installed plugins
    unpack       Unpack packaged plugins
    list         List all installed plugins

Options:
    -h, --help   print help
```

As you can see in Figure 9-2, bin/logstash-plugin -h shows the list of options provided by the script.

Figure 9-2. *Options provided by* logstash-plugin

Listing Logstash Plug-ins

Logstash provides an option to list all of the plug-ins currently available. To list the plug-ins, issue the following command:

```
[vishne0@centylog logstash]$ bin/logstash-plugin list

logstash-codec-collectd
logstash-codec-dots
logstash-codec-edn
logstash-codec-edn_lines
logstash-codec-es_bulk
logstash-codec-fluent
logstash-codec-graphite
logstash-codec-json
logstash-codec-json_lines
logstash-codec-line
logstash-codec-msgpack
logstash-codec-multiline
logstash-codec-netflow
logstash-codec-oldlogstashjson
logstash-codec-plain
logstash-codec-rubydebug
logstash-filter-anonymize
logstash-filter-checksum
logstash-filter-clone
logstash-filter-csv
logstash-filter-date
logstash-filter-dns
logstash-filter-drop
logstash-filter-fingerprint
logstash-filter-geoip
logstash-filter-grok
logstash-filter-json
logstash-filter-kv
logstash-filter-metrics
logstash-filter-multiline
logstash-filter-mutate
logstash-filter-ruby
logstash-filter-sleep
logstash-filter-split
logstash-filter-syslog_pri
logstash-filter-throttle
logstash-filter-urldecode
logstash-filter-useragent
logstash-filter-uuid
logstash-filter-xml
logstash-input-beats
logstash-input-couchdb_changes
logstash-input-elasticsearch
logstash-input-eventlog
logstash-input-exec
```

```
logstash-input-file
logstash-input-ganglia
logstash-input-gelf
logstash-input-generator
logstash-input-graphite
logstash-input-heartbeat
logstash-input-http
logstash-input-http_poller
logstash-input-imap
logstash-input-irc
logstash-input-jdbc
logstash-input-kafka
logstash-input-log4j
logstash-input-lumberjack
logstash-input-pipe
logstash-input-rabbitmq
logstash-input-redis
logstash-input-s3
logstash-input-snmptrap
logstash-input-sqs
logstash-input-stdin
logstash-input-syslog
logstash-input-tcp
logstash-input-twitter
logstash-input-udp
logstash-input-unix
logstash-input-xmpp
logstash-input-zeromq
logstash-output-cloudwatch
logstash-output-csv
logstash-output-elasticsearch
logstash-output-email
logstash-output-exec
logstash-output-file
logstash-output-ganglia
logstash-output-gelf
logstash-output-graphite
logstash-output-hipchat
logstash-output-http
logstash-output-irc
logstash-output-juggernaut
logstash-output-kafka
logstash-output-lumberjack
logstash-output-nagios
logstash-output-nagios_nsca
logstash-output-null
logstash-output-opentsdb
logstash-output-pagerduty
logstash-output-pipe
logstash-output-rabbitmq
logstash-output-redis
logstash-output-s3
```

```
logstash-output-sns
logstash-output-sqs
logstash-output-statsd
logstash-output-stdout
logstash-output-tcp
logstash-output-udp
logstash-output-xmpp
logstash-output-zeromq
logstash-patterns-core
```

Figure 9-3 shows the list of all of the plug-ins available for Logstash.

Figure 9-3. *The Logstash plug-in list*

You can also see the plug-ins versions by running the following command (Figure 9-4):

```
[vishne0@centylog logstash]$ bin/logstash-plugin list --verbose

logstash-codec-collectd (2.0.4)
logstash-codec-dots (2.0.4)
logstash-codec-edn (2.0.4)
logstash-codec-edn_lines (2.0.4)
logstash-codec-es_bulk (2.0.4)
logstash-codec-fluent (2.0.4)
logstash-codec-graphite (2.0.4)
```

```
logstash-codec-json (2.1.4)
logstash-codec-json_lines (2.1.3)
logstash-codec-line (2.1.2)
```

```
[vishne0@centylog logstash]$ bin/logstash-plugin list --verbose

logstash-codec-collectd (2.0.4)
logstash-codec-dots (2.0.4)
logstash-codec-edn (2.0.4)
logstash-codec-edn_lines (2.0.4)
logstash-codec-es_bulk (2.0.4)
logstash-codec-fluent (2.0.4)
logstash-codec-graphite (2.0.4)
logstash-codec-json (2.1.4)
logstash-codec-json_lines (2.1.3)
logstash-codec-line (2.1.2)
logstash-codec-msgpack (2.0.4)
logstash-codec-multiline (2.0.11)
logstash-codec-netflow (2.1.0)
logstash-codec-oldlogstashjson (2.0.4)
logstash-codec-plain (2.0.4)
logstash-codec-rubydebug (2.0.7)
logstash-filter-anonymize (2.0.4)
logstash-filter-checksum (2.0.4)
logstash-filter-clone (2.0.6)
logstash-filter-csv (2.1.3)
logstash-filter-date (2.1.6)
logstash-filter-dns (2.1.3)
logstash-filter-drop (2.0.4)
logstash-filter-fingerprint (2.0.5)
logstash-filter-geoip (2.0.7)
logstash-filter-grok (2.0.5)
logstash-filter-json (2.0.6)
logstash-filter-kv (2.1.0)
logstash-filter-metrics (3.0.2)
logstash-filter-multiline (2.0.5)
logstash-filter-mutate (2.0.6)
logstash-filter-ruby (2.0.5)
logstash-filter-sleep (2.0.4)
logstash-filter-split (2.0.5)
logstash-filter-syslog_pri (2.0.4)
logstash-filter-throttle (2.0.4)
logstash-filter-urldecode (2.0.4)
logstash-filter-useragent (2.0.8)
logstash-filter-uuid (2.0.5)
logstash-filter-xml (2.2.0)
```

Figure 9-4. *The output of* logstash-plugin *in verbose mode*

Installing Logstash Plug-ins

Installing Logstash plug-ins is easy. All you need is a working Internet connection, and you will be able to install the plug-in from the repository hosted by https://rubygems.org. Thus, for example, if you want to install the logstash-input-http plug-in (Figure 9-5), issue the following commands:

```
[vishne0@centylog logstash]$ sudo bin/logstash-plugin install logstash-input-http
Validating logstash-input-http
Installing logstash-input-http
Installation successful
[vishne0@centylog logstash]$ ▮
```

Figure 9-5. *Installing the Logstash plug-in*

```
vishne0@centylog logstash]$ sudo bin/logstash-plugin install logstash-input-http
Validating logstash-input-http
Installing logstash-input-http
Installation successful
```

130

Updating Plug-ins

Updating a plug-in is very important, because if you are using the RPM/DEB-based distribution, when you update Logstash, sometimes the newer version does not come with certain plug-ins that you may have installed previously. If you just need to update one or a few plug-ins, you can update them by name, as follows:

```
[vishne0@centylog logstash]$ sudo bin/logstash-plugin update logstash-input-http
```

This command will update logstash-input-http, if there is an update available for it. If you want to update all the plug-ins, you have to run the following command:

```
[vishne0@centylog logstash]$ sudo bin/logstash-plugin update
```

There may be a situation in which some users might see a message about the version incompatibility of the plug-ins. In such cases, do not update the plug-in. Wait for the repos to be updated with the new compatible version.

If you do not want to verify the updates, you can run the update command with the --no-verify option, as follows:

```
[vishne0@centylog logstash]$ sudo bin/logstash-plugin update --no-verify
```

Removing Plug-ins

To remove a plug-in, run the following command:

```
[vishne0@centylog logstash]$ bin/logstash-plugin uninstall logstash-input-http
```

Logstash Input Plug-ins

Using input plug-ins, Logstash can read events from a specific source. There are lots of input plug-ins available. I will address a few of those that are relevant to this book, as indicated in Table 9-1.

Table 9-1. Logstash Input Plug-ins

Plug-in	Description
Beats	Receives events from the Elastic Beats framework
Elasticsearch	Reads query results from an Elasticsearch cluster
File	Streams events from files
Graphite	Reads metrics from the Graphite tool
HTTP	Receives events over HTTP or HTTPS
Stdin	Reads events from standard input
Syslog	Reads syslog messages as events

Beats Input Plug-in

We used this input plug-in previously in Chapter 4, when we were receiving inputs to Logstash using Filebeat. Required configuration options are as follows:

```
beats {
    port => ...
}
```

Let's review the example that we configured earlier in Chapter 4 (see also Figure 9-6).

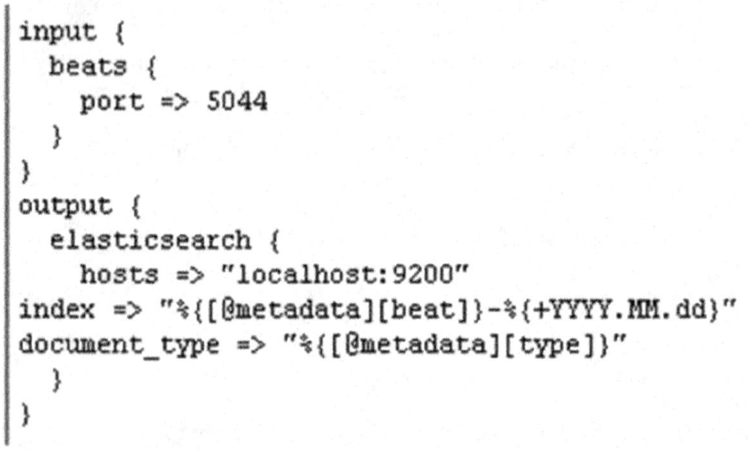

```
input {
  beats {
    port => 5044
  }
}
output {
  elasticsearch {
    hosts => "localhost:9200"
index => "%{[@metadata][beat]}-%{+YYYY.MM.dd}"
document_type => "%{[@metadata][type]}"
  }
}
```

Figure 9-6. *Example of Beats plug-in used in Chapter 4*

```
input {
  beats {
    port => 5044
  }
}

output {
  elasticsearch {
    hosts => "localhost:9200"
index => "%{[@metadata][beat]}-%{+YYYY.MM.dd}"
    document_type => "%{[@metadata][type]}"
  }
}
```

The Beats input plug-in offers the configuration options shown in Table 9-2.

Table 9-2. *Beats Input Plug-in Configuration Options*

Configuration Options	Description

add_field	Adds a field to an event. For example:
	add_field =>{
	"logs" => "beats"
	}
	The value type should be hash.

codec	A codec used for input data. It can be used both for input and output. For example, the Graphite codec reads Graphite-formatted lines.
congestion_threshold	You can use this if something is taking a lot of time to process. Using this option, you can invoke a timeout, such as when something is blocking the Logstash pipeline.
host	IP address or hostname on which to listen
port	The port number on which to listen
ssl	This option can be used to encrypt plain text traffic.
ssl_certificate	Identifies which SSL certificate to use
ssl_certificate_authorities	Used to validate the certificate
ssl_key	The key used for SSL
ssl_verify_mode	Used for server verification of the client
tags	Adds any number of tags for your events
target_field_for_codec	The default field to which the codec will be applied
type	Adds a type field to your events for a specific input

Elasticsearch Input Plug-in

To read existing data, you can use the Elasticsearch input plug-in from an existing Elasticsearch cluster or index. For example, in your configuration file, you can use the following code:

```
input {
  elasticsearch {
   hosts => ["localhost"]
   index => "logstash"
  }
}
```

Here, we are reading data of the index "logstash" on localhost. This code will run a match_all query on all of the documents of the index "logstash".

If you can't do a match to a specific query, for example, if you were indexing apache_access logs, you would want to match the query for code 404. In that case, you can use a query syntax.

```
query => '{ "query": { "match": { "statuscode": 404 } } }'
```

The correct way to include it in the configuration file is as follows:

```
input {
  elasticsearch {
    hosts => ["localhost"]
    query => '{ "query": { "match": { "statuscode": 404 } } }'
    index => "logstash"
  }
}
```

This will now match the query status code 404, but only in all of the documents of the index, as shown in Table 9-3.

Table 9-3. *Elasticsearch Input Plug-in Configuration Options*

Configuration Options	Description
add_field	Simply adds an event to a field
ca_file	SSL certificate authority file
codec	A codec used for input data
docinfo	If this is set, you should include Elasticsearch document information, such as index, type, and the ID in the event
docinfo_fields	List of document metadata
docinfo_target	Where to move the Elasticsearch document info
hosts	List of Elasticsearch hosts to be used for querying
index	The index to search
password	Password authentication
query	Query to execute for a specific value
scan	This enables the Elasticsearch scan search type.
scroll	This controls the keep alive time in seconds for the scrolling request.
size	This option can be used to specify the maximum number of hits per scroll.
ssl	Used to enable SSL
type	Lets you add a type field to any of your events
tags	Adds any number of arbitrary tags
user	A basic authentication

File Input Plug-in

A File input plug-in reads a file such as `tail` in GNU/Linux systems, but it reads the file from beginning. The configuration options are shown in Table 9-4.

```
file {
    path => ...
}
```

Table 9-4. *File Input Plug-in Configuration Options*

Configuration Options	Description
add_field	Simply adds an event to a field
close_older	The file input closes any files that were last read in the specified timespan (in seconds ago). The default is one hour.
codec	A codec used for input data
delimiter	Sets the new line delimiter. Defaults to "\n".
discover_interval	How often (in seconds) we expand the file name patterns in the path option to discover new files to watch.
exclude	Allows you to exclude the file types using this configuration
ignore_older	When the file input discovers a file that was last modified before the specified timespan in seconds, the file is ignored.
max_open_files	Specifies the maximum number of file handles this input consumes at any one time
path	Specifies the path of a file, for example, /var/log/httpd/access_log
sincedb_path	This input type can specify the path of the sincedb database file. It resides in the user's home directory, for example, /home/vishne0/.sincedb.
sincedb_write_interval	Specifies a time interval for writing to the sincedb database
start_position	With this input, you can specify from where Logstash starts reading the file—from the beginning or from the end.
stat_interval	Allows you to specify the time period to stat files, to see if they have been modified
type	Used to add a type field to any of your events
tags	Adds any number of arbitrary tags to your event

See the following for a more realistic example, as used in earlier chapters:

```
input {
    file {
        path => "/var/log/httpd/error.log"
        start_position => "beginning"
      type => "logs"
    }
}
```

Make sure that user logstash has permission to access the logfile. To do this, just run the following command:

```
[vishne0@centylog ~]$ setfacl -m u:logstash:r /var/log/httpd/error_log
```

This will give user logstash permission to read the error_log file.

Graphite Input Plug-in

The required configuration options for the Graphite input plug-in are as follows:

```
graphite {
    port => ...
}
```

A more realistic example is as follows:

```
input {
  graphite {
    port => 2003
    type => "graphite"
}
```

The Graphite input plug-in configuration options are shown in Table 9-5.

Table 9-5. *Graphite Input Plug-in Configuration Options*

Configuration Options	Description
add_field	Simply adds an event to a field
codec	A codec used for input data
host	Used to specify the host
mode	Provides values server, client. The default value is server.
port	Used to specify the port number
ssl_cert	The value type here should be the path to the SSL certificate.
ssl_enable	Used to enable SSL
ssl_extra_chain_cert	An array of extra certificates
ssl_key	Used to provide an SSL key
ssl_key_passpharse	Used to provide an SSL password
ssl_verify	Used to verify the identity of the SSL certificate
stat_interval	Allows you to specify the time period to stat files, to see if they have been modified
type	Adds a type field to any of your events
tags	Adds any number of arbitrary tags to your event

HTTP Input Plug-in

The Logstash HTTP input plug-in can be used to send signals of multiline events over HTTP(S). This HTTP input plug-in can also be used to receive webhook requests from other applications. It also supports basic HTTP authentication. You can also use SSL and send data encrypted over HTTPS.

The HTTP input plug-in required option is as follows:

```
Input {
http {
host => "0.0.0.0" # default
    port => 8080 # default
  }
}
```

The HTTP input plug-in configuration options are shown in Table 9-6.

Table 9-6. *The HTTP Input Plug-in Configuration Options*

Configuration Options	Description
add_field	Simply adds an event to a field
codec	A codec used for input data
additional_codecs	With this, you can apply specific codecs for specific content types.
host	Codec used to decode the incoming data
port	Used to specify port number
keystore	The JKS keystore used to validate the client's certificates
keystore_password	Sets the truststore password
password	Basic password authentication
port	The port to bind to
response_headers	Specifies a set of custom headers
user	Specifies username for authentication
verify_mode	Set this option to verify the client certificate method.
type	Allows you to add a type field to any of your events
tags	Adds any number of arbitrary tags to your event
threads	The maximum number of threads to use

Stdin Input Plug-in

The Stdin input plug-in reads events from standard output. You used the Stdin input plug-in in Chapter 1. Note the following example:

```
[vishne0@centylog ~]$ ./logstash -e 'input { stdin { } } output { stdout {} }'
Required configuration options
stdin {
}
```

The Stdin input plug-in configuration options are shown in Table 9-7.

Table 9-7. *Stdin Input Plug-in Configuration Options*

Configuration Options	Description
add_field	Simply adds an event to a field
codec	A codec used for input data
tags	Adds any number of arbitrary tags to your event
type	Allows you to add a type field to any of your events

Syslog Input Plug-in

The Syslog input plug-in is very useful, as Syslog runs on every GNU/Linux machine. With the Syslog input plug-in, you can read events from network devices. The Syslog input only supports RFC3164. For more information on RFC, visit www.ietf.org/rfc/rfc3164.txt. The perfect way to use this plug-in is for a setup in which you have too many servers, and you want them all to send their inputs from Syslog to the centralized logging server. On the centralized logging server, you can configure Logstash to read the events from Syslog.

The Syslog input plug-in required configuration is as follows:

```
        syslog {
}
```

A more realistic example of this is as follows:

```
input {
  syslog {
    type => syslog
    port => 514
  }
```

The Syslog input plug-in configuration options are shown in Table 9-8.

Table 9-8. *The Syslog Input Plug-in Configuration Options*

Configuration Options	Description
add_field	Simply adds an event to a field
codec	A codec used for input data
facility_labels	Default values are: "kernel", "user-level", "mail", "system", "security/authorization", "syslogd", "line printer", "network news", "UUCP", "clock", "security/authorization", "FTP", "NTP", "log audit", "log alert", "clock", "local0", "local1", "local2", "local3", "local4", "local5", "local6", and "local7". These labels are defined in RFC3164.

(*continued*)

Table 9-8. (*continued*)

Configuration Options	Description
host	The IP address listened to
locale	Used to specify a locale to be used for date parsing, using either a IETF-BCP47 or POSIX language tag
port	The port to listen on
severity_labels	Labels for severity levels, as defined in RFC3164
timezone	Used to specify a time zone canonical ID to be employed for date parsing
tags	Adds any number of arbitrary tags to your event
type	Allows you to add a type field to any of your events
use_labels	Use label parsing for severity and facility levels

Logstash Output Plug-ins

As in the case of input plug-ins, Logstash provides many output plug-ins as well. An *output plug-in* is used to send the data to a specific destination.

You have used a few output plug-ins in previous chapters, including:

- Elasticsearch output plug-in, in Chapter 3

- Graphite output plug-in, in Chapter 6

You will now learn about the output plug-ins that are relevant to this book, as described in Table 9-9.

Table 9-9. *Logstash Output Plug-ins*

Plug-ins	Description
Elasticsearch	Stores logs in Elasticsearch
File	Writes events to a file
Graphite	Writes metrics to Graphite
Syslog	Sends events to a Syslog server
Stdout	Sends events to a Syslog server
	Print events to standard output

Elasticsearch Output Plug-in

You used this output plug-in in Chapter 3. The Elasticsearch output plug-in stores logs in Elasticsearch, and as we are also using Kibana in this book, you must retrieve the output using the plug-in.

The plug-in supports the following configuration option:

```
elasticsearch {
}
```

The more realistic example used in Chapter 3 is shown here:

```
output {
  elasticsearch {
    hosts => ["localhost:9200"]
    user => es_admin
    password => admin123
  }
  stdout { codec => rubydebug }
}
```

The Elasticsearch output plug-in configuration options are shown in Table 9-10.

Table 9-10. *Elasticsearch Ouput Plug-in Configuration Options*

Configuration Options	Description
action	To perform an action, the default values are index, delete, create, and update
cacert	Validates the server certificate by providing a .cer or .pem file
codec	A codec used for data output
doc_as_upsert	Enables it for update mode
document_id	The document ID for the index
document_type	The document type to write events to
flush_size	The plug-in uses the bulk index API for improved indexing performance.
hosts	Sets the host(s) of the remote instance
idle_flush_time	The amount of time since the last flush before a flush is forced
index	The index used to write the events
keystore	The keystore used to present a certificate to the server
keystore_password	Sets the password
manage_template	Unless you set up the option manage_template, a default mapping template will apply, such as logstash-%{+YYYY.MM.dd.
parent	For child documents, the ID of the associated parent
password	Authenticates the Elasticsearch user with a password
path	The path at which the Elasticsearch server lives
proxy	Sets the address of a forward HTTP proxy
retry_max_interval	Sets the maximum interval between bulk retries
routing	A routing override to be applied to all processed events
script	Sets the script name for scripted update mode
script_lang	Sets the language of the script used
script_type	Defines the type of script referenced by the script variable inline
script_var_name	Sets the variable name passed to the script
scripted_upsert	If enabled, the script is in charge of creating a nonexistent document.

(continued)

Table 9-10. (*continued*)

Configuration Options	Description
sniffing	This setting asks Elasticsearch for the list of all cluster nodes and adds them to the hosts list.
sniffing_delay	How long to wait, in seconds, between sniffing attempts
ssl	Enables an SSL/TLS-secured communication to an Elasticsearch cluster
ssl_certificate_verification	Option to validate the server's certificate
template	You can set up your own path with this option.
template_name	This configuration option defines how the template is named inside Elasticsearch.
template_overwrite	The template_overwrite option will always overwrite the indicated template in Elasticsearch with either the one indicated by the template or the one included.
timeout	Sets the timeout for network operations and requests sent to Elasticsearch
truststore	The JKS truststore to validate the server's certificate. Use either :truststore or :cacert.
truststore_password	Sets the truststore password
upsert	Sets upsert content for update mode. Create a new document with this parameter as a json string if document_id doesn't exist.
user	Username to authenticate a user for Elasticsearch
workers	The number of workers to use for this output

File Output Plug-in

The file output plug-in writes events to files on disk. You have to specify the path to the files for the events to be stored. The required configuration option is as follows:

```
file {
    path => ...
}
```

The more realistic example of the configuration that you saw in Chapter 3 follows:

```
input {
file {
path => "/var/log/httpd/access_log"
start_position => "beginning"
}
}
```

The File output plug-in configuration options are shown in Table 9-11.

Table 9-11. *The File Output Plug-in Configuration Options*

Configuration Options	Description
codec	The codec used for the data output
create_if_deleted	If the file is deleted and the event is coming and has to be stored in the file, it will create the file again.
dir_mode	Directory access mode to use
file_mode	File access mode to use
filename_failure	If the generated path is invalid, the events will be saved into this file, inside the defined path.
flush_interval	Flush interval for flushing writes to log files
gzip	Compresses the output in gzip before writing to disk
path	The path to the file to write
workers	The number of workers to use for this output

Graphite Output Plug-in

With the Graphite output plug-in, you can take the inputs from any log files and pass them to Graphite. The required configuration is as follows:

```
graphite {
}
```

You used the following code in Chapter 4 with the Graphite output:

```
output {
    graphite {
        fields_are_metrics => true
        include_metrics => ["^apache\.response\..*"]
        host => "localhost"
        port => "2003"
    }
}
```

The Graphite output plug-in configuration options are shown in Table 9-12.

Table 9-12. *The Graphite Output Plug-in Configuration Options*

Configuration Options	Description
codec	The codec used for the data output
exclude_metrics	Use this to exclude a metric.
field_are_metrics	An array indicating that these event fields should be treated as metrics and will be sent to Graphite
host	Hostname
include_metrics	Include only regex-matched metric names
metrics	Used for metric names and values. For example, you have used the following in Chapter 6: metrics { meter => "apache.response.%{host}.%{response}"
metrics_format	Defines the format of the metric string
nested_object_separated	
port	Port to connect to Graphite server
reconnect_interval	Interval between reconnect attempts to Carbon
resend_on_failure	Indicates that metrics should be resent, if there is a failure
timestamp_field	Use this field for the timestamp, instead of @timestamp.
workers	The number of workers to use for this output

Syslog Output Plug-in

The Syslog output plug-in isn't supplied by default in Logstash. The plug-in is maintained by the community, and you can use it if you want to send events to Syslog. It will be useful if you want to send some specific device logs or possibly application logs from a remote server.

However, you can install it using the following command:

```
[vishne0@centylog logstash]$ bin/logstash-plugin install logstash-output-syslog
```

The Syslog output plug-in configuration options are shown in Table 9-13.

Table 9-13. The Syslog Ouput Plug-in Configuration Options

Configuration Options	Description
codec	The codec used for the data output
appname	Application name for Syslog messages
facility	Facility label for Syslog messages
host	Syslog server IP to connect to
include_metrics	Include only regex-matched metric names
message	Message text to log
msgid	Message ID for Syslog
port	Syslog server port to connect to
procid	Process ID for Syslog messages
protocol	Syslog server protocol
rfc	Syslog message format you can use: RFC3164 or RFC5424
severity	Severity label for Syslog. For example, warning, critical, error, and so on
sourcehost	Source host for Syslog messages
workers	The number of workers to use for this output

Stdout Output Plug-in

You can use this simple plug-in to print Stdout. The output is helpful for debugging. In earlier chapters, you used Stdout in your configuration files, using the following configuration:

```
output {
  stdout { codec => rubydebug }
}
```

Required configuration options are:

```
stdout {
}
```

Stdout output plug-in configuration options are shown in Table 9-14.

Table 9-14. Stdout Output Plug-in Configuration Options

Configuration Options	Description
codec	The codec used for the data output
workers	The number of workers to use for this output

Summary

In this chapter, you learned about Logstash plug-ins. You also learned about how input and output plug-ins work and about their configuration options, using some realistic examples of configurations in previous chapters.

In the next chapter, you will see how to integrate Logstash with the Puppet and Foreman configuration-management tool.

■ ■ ■

## CHAPTER 10

Managing the ELK Stack with Puppet and Foreman

At this point, you have learned about the ELK Stack in depth. Next let's move on to how to use a configuration-management tool and how you can build the ELK Stack setup using the tool. The configuration-management tool is called Puppet, from Puppet Labs, and server administrators use it to automate, configure, and manage server infrastructure.

A well-executed plan using Puppet gives you a lot more time to work on other aspects of server infrastructure, such as hardening security or scaling the infrastructure, rather than spending time on configuration or updating the servers.

Puppet comes in two versions: Puppet Enterprise and open source Puppet. Puppet can be installed on any GNU/Linux distribution. Puppet works in a Master/Agent setup: Puppet master is the main server that controls the nodes that you then use to call Puppet agents.

At this point, you have a working ELK Stack setup running. In this chapter, you are going to configure Foreman and Puppet. To do so, you have to get two new freshly installed servers, either CentOS 7 or Ubuntu 16.04.1 LTS, as you prefer. For the setup, you must have at least two servers: Puppet master and Puppet node.

Installing Puppet and configuring Puppet agents is quite complicated. You will use Foreman. Foreman is an open source project that helps administrators manage servers, including configuring, updating, and monitoring them. Using Foreman, you can automate tasks and install applications. Foreman comes with a useful GUI interface, and it is very easy to configure. For more information on Foreman, visit https://theforeman.org.

Installing Foreman on CentOS 7

Prerequisites

To begin installing Puppet master, you have to make sure that your hostname is set up, or Foreman will not install and return an error. You will set up a demo hostname, so that the Foreman installer doesn't return any errors. To check your hostname, issue the following command:

```
[vishneo@localhost ~]$ hostname -f
localhost
```

As you can see in Figure 10-1, it returned localhost as hostname. You must change it, however. Change the /etc/hosts file, as follows:

```
[vishneo@localhost ~]$ sudo vi /etc/hosts
Inside the hosts file I have below content
```

```
127.0.0.1    localhost localhost.localdomain localhost4 localhost4.localdomain4
::1          localhost localhost.localdomain localhost6 localhost6.localdomain6
~
~
```

Figure 10-1. *The content of the* /etc/hosts *file*

You have to add one more entry, to make sure that you have your hostname set up properly, as shown in Figure 10-2. If you already have a public IP and a complete DNS setup, you can go ahead and skip this part.

```
127.0.0.1    localhost localhost.localdomain localhost4 localhost4.localdomain4
::1          localhost localhost.localdomain localhost6 localhost6.localdomain6
192.168.1.103 puppet.centylabs.com puppet
```

Figure 10-2. *Hostname added to* /etc/hosts

As shown in Figure 10-2, I have added a hostname for my server. I am using a server from Linode, so that's why it's named puppet.centylabs.com. Remember, this is just a demo hostname. Once this is complete, you will add an entry in /etc/hostname, as follows:

```
[vishne0@localhost ~]$ sudo vi /etc/hostname
```

Remove localhost entry and add puppet in your /etc/hostname at the top. Save the file, press :wq, and exit the vi editor.

Now run the following command, to check the hostname:

```
[vishne0@localhost ~]$ hostnamectl
[vishne0@localhost etc]$ hostnamectl
   Static hostname: puppet
Transient hostname: puppet
localhost.localdomain
          Icon name: computer-vm
            Chassis: vm
         Machine ID: 72863e389b584a4dab36fae7f3bffda2
            Boot ID: 87603902f29c4eaba9f312d1f5b06a1d
   Operating System: CentOS Linux 7 (Core)
        CPE OS Name: cpe:/o:centos:centos:7
             Kernel: Linux 4.7.0-x86_64-linode72
       Architecture: x86_64
```

As you can see, it shows the hostname that you have just set up. Because the hostname is set up correctly, we will now move ahead and install Foreman. Another important point here is that you must have at least 4GB of RAM and 2GB of hard drive. Visit this page for Foreman hardware requirements: https://theforeman.org/manuals/1.13/index.html#3.1.2HardwareRequirements.

Finally, as these are new systems, we need to ensure that the firewall configuration is running and allowing the connection to the ports of the various services installed in this chapter. The subject of the firewall configuration and the strengthening of the system should be properly addressed for a production system, but for this system, the following commands will produce a working configuration.

For Centos:

```
firewall-cmd --permanent --zone=public --add-port=22/tcp
firewall-cmd --permanent --zone=public --add-port=443/tcp
firewall-cmd --permanent --zone=public --add-port=5601/tcp
firewall-cmd --reload
```

For Ubuntu:

```
ufw allow 22/tcp
ufw allow 443/tcp
ufw allow 5601/tcp
ufw enable
```

Adding Repositories

First, you have to add the EPEL repository on CentOS 7 (Figure 10-3), as follows:

```
[vishne0@puppet ~]$ sudo rpm -ivh https://dl.fedoraproject.org/pub/epel/epel-release-
latest-7.noarch.rpm Retrieving https://dl.fedoraproject.org/pub/epel/epel-release-latest-7.
noarch.rpm
warning: /var/tmp/rpm-tmp.HDaJol: Header V3 RSA/SHA256 Signature, key ID 352c64e5: NOKEY
Preparing...                           ################################# [100%]
Updating / installing...
   1:epel-release-7-8                   ################################# [100%]
```

```
[vishne0@puppet ~]$ sudo rpm -ivh https://dl.fedoraproject.org/pub/epel/epel-release-latest-7.noarch.rpm
[sudo] password for vishne0:
Retrieving https://dl.fedoraproject.org/pub/epel/epel-release-latest-7.noarch.rpm
warning: /var/tmp/rpm-tmp.HDaJol: Header V3 RSA/SHA256 Signature, key ID 352c64e5: NOKEY
Preparing...                           ################################# [100%]
Updating / installing...
   1:epel-release-7-8                   ################################# [100%]
```

Figure 10-3. *Adding the EPEL repository*

Next, you will add the Puppet4 and Foreman repositories, as follows:

```
[vishne0@puppet ~]$ sudo rpm -ivh https://yum.puppetlabs.com/puppetlabs-release-pc1-el-7.
noarch.rpm
Retrieving http://yum.puppetlabs.com/puppetlabs-release-el-7.noarch.rpm
warning: /var/tmp/rpm-tmp.EASlOg: Header V4 RSA/SHA512 Signature, key ID 4bd6ec30: NOKEY
Preparing...                           ################################# [100%]
Updating / installing...
   1:puppetlabs-release-22.0-2          ################################# [100%]
[vishne0@puppet ~]$ sudo yum  install epel-release https://yum.theforeman.org/
releases/1.13/el7/x86_64/foreman-release.rpm
```

All of the repositories are now installed. Run the following command to list them (Figure 10-4).

```
[vishne0@puppet ~]$ sudo yum repolist
Loaded plugins: fastestmirror
foreman                                                                           | 2.9 kB  00:00:00
foreman-plugins                                                                   | 2.9 kB  00:00:00
(1/2): foreman-plugins/x86_64/primary_db                                          |  78 kB  00:00:01
(2/2): foreman/x86_64/primary_db                                                  | 144 kB  00:00:07
Loading mirror speeds from cached hostfile
 * base: mirrors.linode.com
 * epel: epel.mirror.angkasa.id
 * extras: mirrors.linode.com
 * updates: mirrors.linode.com
repo id                          repo name                                            status
base/7/x86_64                    CentOS-7 - Base                                       9,007
epel/x86_64                      Extra Packages for Enterprise Linux 7 - x86_64       10,673
extras/7/x86_64                  CentOS-7 - Extras                                       392
foreman/x86_64                   Foreman 1.13                                            384
foreman-plugins/x86_64           Foreman plugins 1.13                                    259
puppetlabs-pc1/x86_64            Puppet Labs PC1 Repository el 7 - x86_64                 94
updates/7/x86_64                 CentOS-7 - Updates                                    2,507
repolist: 23,316
[vishne0@puppet ~]$
```

Figure 10-4. *The installed repository list*

```
[vishne0@puppet ~]$ sudo yum repolist
```

The next step is to install Foreman. To accomplish this, run the following command:

```
[vishne0@puppet ~]$ sudo yum install foreman-installer
```

```
foreman-installer                    noarch      1:1.13.0-1.el7                foreman           807 k
Installing for dependencies:
 audit-libs-python                   x86_64      2.4.1-5.el7                   base               69 k
 checkpolicy                         x86_64      2.1.12-6.el7                  base              247 k
 foreman-selinux                     noarch      1.13.0-1.el7                  foreman            43 k
 libcgroup                           x86_64      0.41-8.el7                    base               64 k
 libsemanage-python                  x86_64      2.1.10-18.el7                 base               94 k
 libyaml                             x86_64      0.1.4-11.el7_0                base               55 k
 policycoreutils-python              x86_64      2.2.5-20.el7                  base              435 k
 puppet-agent                        x86_64      1.7.0-1.el7                   puppetlabs-pc1     24 M
 python-IPy                          noarch      0.75-6.el7                    base               32 k
 ruby                                x86_64      2.0.0.598-25.el7_1            base               67 k
 ruby-irb                            noarch      2.0.0.598-25.el7_1            base               88 k
 ruby-libs                           x86_64      2.0.0.598-25.el7_1            base              2.8 M
 rubygem-ansi                        noarch      1.4.3-2.el7                   epel               36 k
 rubygem-bigdecimal                  x86_64      1.2.0-25.el7_1                base               79 k
 rubygem-clamp                       noarch      1.0.0-5.el7                   foreman            28 k
 rubygem-hashie                      noarch      2.0.5-4.el7                   foreman            18 k
 rubygem-highline                    noarch      1.6.21-5.el7                  foreman           500 k
 rubygem-io-console                  x86_64      0.4.2-25.el7_1                base               50 k
 rubygem-json                        x86_64      1.7.7-25.el7_1                base               75 k
 rubygem-kafo                        noarch      0.9.6-1.el7                   foreman            58 k
 rubygem-kafo_parsers               noarch      0.1.2-1.el7                   foreman            11 k
 rubygem-kafo_wizards               noarch      0.0.1-2.el7                   foreman            13 k
 rubygem-little-plugger             noarch      1.1.3-21.el7                  foreman            12 k
 rubygem-logging                     noarch      1.8.2-4.el7                   foreman            61 k
 rubygem-multi_json                 noarch      1.10.1-3.el7                  foreman            19 k
 rubygem-powerbar                    noarch      1.0.17-1.el7                  foreman            13 k
 rubygem-psych                       x86_64      2.0.0-25.el7_1                base               77 k
 rubygem-rdoc                        noarch      4.0.0-25.el7_1                base              318 k
 rubygems                            noarch      2.0.14-25.el7_1               base              212 k
 selinux-policy                      noarch      3.13.1-60.el7_2.9             updates           377 k
 selinux-policy-targeted             noarch      3.13.1-60.el7_2.9             updates           3.9 M
 setools-libs                        x86_64      3.3.7-46.el7                  base              485 k

Transaction Summary
================================================================================
Install  1 Package (+32 Dependent packages)

Total download size: 35 M
Installed size: 56 M
Is this ok [y/d/N]: █
```

Figure 10-5. *List of packages and dependencies needed for Foreman*

This will show you a long list of packages and dependencies to be installed (Figure 10-5). Press y, and then Enter, to install everything.

While installing, it will prompt you with a message for accepting the importing key for the repositories.

```
Retrieving key from file:///etc/pki/rpm-gpg/RPM-GPG-KEY-foreman
Importing GPG key 0x7DFE6FC2:
 Userid     : "Foreman Release Signing Key (1.13) <packages@theforeman.org>"
 Fingerprint: 84e7 90df fb1d 2eae c429 c6cd 4ea2 f7e7 7dfe 6fc2
 Package    : foreman-release-1.13.0-1.el7.noarch (@/foreman-release)
 From       : /etc/pki/rpm-gpg/RPM-GPG-KEY-foreman
Is this ok [y/N]: y
Retrieving key from file:///etc/pki/rpm-gpg/RPM-GPG-KEY-puppetlabs-PC1
Importing GPG key 0x4BD6EC30:
 Userid     : "Puppet Labs Release Key (Puppet Labs Release Key) <info@puppetlabs.com>"
 Fingerprint: 47b3 20eb 4c7c 375a a9da e1a0 1054 b7a2 4bd6 ec30
 Package    : puppetlabs-release-pc1-1.1.0-2.el7.noarch (installed)
 From       : /etc/pki/rpm-gpg/RPM-GPG-KEY-puppetlabs-PC1
Is this ok [y/N]: y
Retrieving key from file:///etc/pki/rpm-gpg/RPM-GPG-KEY-puppet-PC1
Importing GPG key 0xEF8D349F:
 Userid     : "Puppet, Inc. Release Key (Puppet, Inc. Release Key) <release@puppet.com>"
 Fingerprint: 6f6b 1550 9cf8 e59e 6e46 9f32 7f43 8280 ef8d 349f
```

```
Package     : puppetlabs-release-pc1-1.1.0-2.el7.noarch (installed)
From        : /etc/pki/rpm-gpg/RPM-GPG-KEY-puppet-PC1
Is this ok [y/N]: y
Retrieving key from file:///etc/pki/rpm-gpg/RPM-GPG-KEY-EPEL-7
Importing GPG key 0x352C64E5:
 Userid     : "Fedora EPEL (7) <epel@fedoraproject.org>"
 Fingerprint: 91e9 7d7c 4a5e 96f1 7f3e 888f 6a2f aea2 352c 64e5
 Package    : epel-release-7-8.noarch (installed)
 From       : /etc/pki/rpm-gpg/RPM-GPG-KEY-EPEL-7
Is this ok [y/N]: y
```

Type y and press Enter for each message. Once complete, Foreman will be installed with all its dependencies. You now run `foreman-installer` to install the required packages (Figure 10-6).

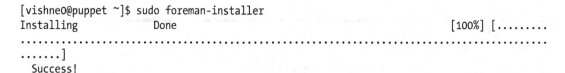

Figure 10-6. `foreman-installer` *installing all of the packages and dependencies*

```
[vishne0@puppet ~]$ sudo foreman-installer
```

As seen in Figure 10-6, you are using `foreman-installer`, which is a collection of Puppet modules. It will install everything required for a working Foreman setup. It uses OS packaging. As we are installing it on CentOS 7, it will use the RPM packages. The installation will take some time to complete.

Once the installation is complete, it shows a message with the following content:

```
[vishne0@puppet ~]$ sudo foreman-installer
Installing             Done                                    [100%] [........
.......................................................................................
.......]
  Success!
```

- Foreman is running at `https://puppet.centylog.com`.

- Initial credentials are `admin/QohXZt7BaaeESFWp`.

- Foreman Proxy is running at `https://puppet.centylog.com:8443`.

- Puppet master is running at port 8140.

- The full log is at `/var/log/foreman-installer/foreman-installer.log`.

Save the details, as you will need them to log into Foreman. Now simply access the Foreman admin page at `https://yourip`. As Foreman is using a Puppet SSL certificate, it will display a certificate not valid warning. Just accept it as valid. You can remove the warning by installing a signed SSL certificate for your domain. The login page looks like the one shown in Figure 10-7.

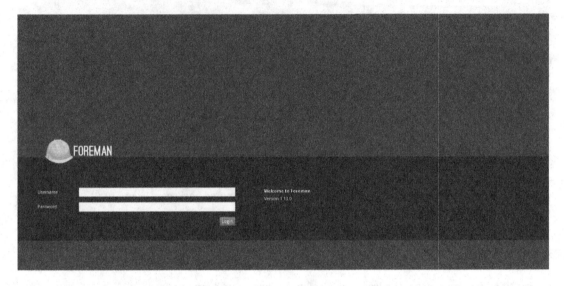

Figure 10-7. *Foreman login screen*

Installing Foreman on Ubuntu 16.04.1 LTS

Before proceeding with the installation of Foreman on Ubuntu 16.04.1, you have to set up the hostname, as you did with CentOS 7 (Figure 10-8). Run the following command:

```
vishne0@ubuntu:~$ sudo vi /etc/hosts
```

```
127.0.0.1        localhost
127.0.1.1        ubuntu.members.linode.com        ubuntu
192.168.1.203    puppet.ubulogy.com puppet

::1      localhost ip6-localhost ip6-loopback
ff02::1 ip6-allnodes
ff02::2 ip6-allrouters
```

Figure 10-8. *Adding a hostname in the* /etc/hosts *file on Ubuntu 16.04.1 LTS*

Change the hostname in /etc/hostname as well, as shown here:

```
vishne0@ubuntu:~$ sudo vi /etc/hostname
```

In the hostname, I have removed the default hostname and entered puppet. Verify if the hostname has changed, as follows:

```
vishne0@puppet:~$ sudo hostnamectl
[sudo] password for vishne0:
   Static hostname: puppet
        Icon name: computer-vm
```

```
        Chassis: vm
     Machine ID: XXXXXXXXXXXXXXXXXXXXXXXXXXXXXXXX
        Boot ID: XXXXXXXXXXXXXXXXXXXXXXXXXXXXXXXX
 Virtualization: qemu
Operating System: Ubuntu 16.04.1 LTS
         Kernel: Linux 4.6.5-x86_64-linode71
   Architecture: x86-64
```

The hostname is changed, so now let's move ahead and install Foreman. To install Foreman, issue the following commands:

```
vishne0@ubuntu:~$ wget https://apt.puppetlabs.com/puppetlabs-release-pc1-xenial.deb
vishne0@ubuntu:~$ sudo dpkg -i puppetlabs-release-pc1-xenial.debvishne0@ubuntu:~$ sudo dpkg
-i puppetlabs-release-pc1-xenial.deb
```

Now let's enable the repositories (see also Figure 10-9).

```
vishne0@ubuntu:/$ echo "deb http://deb.theforeman.org/ xenial 1.13" | sudo tee -a /etc/apt/
sources.list.d/foreman.list
vishne0@ubuntu:/$ echo "deb http://deb.theforeman.org/ plugins 1.13" | sudo tee -a /etc/apt/
sources.list.d/foreman.list
vishne0@puppet:~$ wget -q https://deb.theforeman.org/pubkey.gpg -O- | apt-key add -
```

```
vishne0@ubuntu:/$ echo "deb http://deb.theforeman.org/ xenial 1.13" | sudo tee -a /etc/apt/sources.list.d/foreman.list
deb http://deb.theforeman.org/ xenial 1.13
vishne0@ubuntu:/$ echo "deb http://deb.theforeman.org/ plugins 1.13" | sudo tee -a /etc/apt/sources.list.d/foreman.list
deb http://deb.theforeman.org/ plugins 1.13
```

Figure 10-9. Adding repositories and keys on Ubuntu 16.04.1 LTS

Let's install Foreman (Figure 10-10) using the following command:

```
vishne0@puppet:~$ sudo apt-get update && sudo apt-get install foreman-installer
```

```
vishne0@ubuntu:/$ sudo apt-get install foreman-installer
Reading package lists... Done
Building dependency tree
Reading state information... Done
The following additional packages will be installed:
  fonts-lato javascript-common libjs-jquery libruby2.3 libyaml-0-2 puppet-agent rake ruby ruby-ansi ruby-clamp ruby-did-you-mean ruby-hashie ruby-highline ruby-kafo
  ruby-kafo-parsers ruby-kafo-wizards ruby-little-plugger ruby-logging ruby-minitest ruby-multi-json ruby-net-telnet ruby-oj ruby-power-assert ruby-powerbar
  ruby-test-unit ruby2.3 rubygems-integration unzip zip
Suggested packages:
  apache2 | lighttpd | httpd ri ruby-dev ruby-activesupport bundler
The following NEW packages will be installed:
  fonts-lato foreman-installer javascript-common libjs-jquery libruby2.3 libyaml-0-2 puppet-agent rake ruby ruby-ansi ruby-clamp ruby-did-you-mean ruby-hashie
  ruby-highline ruby-kafo ruby-kafo-parsers ruby-kafo-wizards ruby-little-plugger ruby-logging ruby-minitest ruby-multi-json ruby-net-telnet ruby-oj ruby-power-assert
  ruby-powerbar ruby-test-unit ruby2.3 rubygems-integration unzip zip
0 upgraded, 30 newly installed, 0 to remove and 0 not upgraded.
Need to get 21.2 MB of archives.
After this operation, 116 MB of additional disk space will be used.
Do you want to continue? [Y/n] y
WARNING: The following packages cannot be authenticated!
  ruby-kafo-parsers ruby-kafo-wizards ruby-kafo foreman-installer
Install these packages without verification? [y/N]
```

Figure 10-10. Installing Foreman on Ubuntu 16.04.1 LTS

While installing Foreman, it will ask you to authenticate a few Ruby packages (Figure 10-11). Just type y and press Enter.

```
vishne0@puppet:~$ sudo foreman-installer

Installing              Debug: /Stage[main]/Foreman::Database::Postgresql/ [51%] [...........................................
```

***Figure 10-11.** Installing packages needed by Foreman*

Now run `foreman-installer`.

```
vishne0@puppet:~$ sudo foreman-installer
```

Once the installation is complete, it will display these details:

- Foreman is running at `https://puppet.ubulogy.com`.

- Initial credentials are `admin/t75CxjMohLop5vd9`.

- Foreman Proxy is running at `https://puppet.ubulogy.com:8443`.

- Puppet master is running at port 8140.

- The full log is at `/var/log/foreman-installer/foreman.log`.

As mentioned earlier, access Foreman using your hostname, if you have a valid name server, or use your public IP: `https://yourpublicip`. As Foreman is using a puppet SSL certificate, it will display a certificate not valid warning. Just accept it as valid. You can remove the warning by installing a signed SSL certificate for your domain.

As shown in Figure 10-12, Foreman is running on the Ubuntu server.

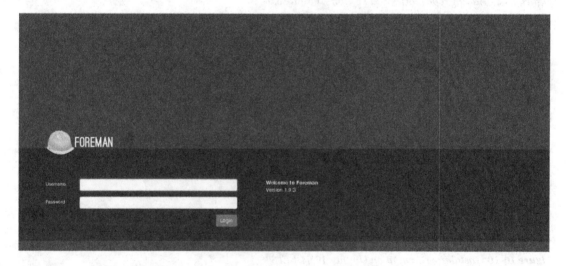

***Figure 10-12.** Foreman running on Ubuntu 16.04.1*

Now let's go back to the CentOS 7 server on which you installed Foreman earlier. Before logging in, run the Puppet agent, to add the server itself, as it's the first host. Change the directory to /opt/puppetlabs and issue the following command:

```
[vishne0@puppet puppetlabs]$ sudo bin/puppet agent --test [sudo]
password for vishne0:
Info: Retrieving pluginfacts
Info: Retrieving plugin
Info: Caching catalog for puppet.centylog.com
Info: Applying configuration version '1473158139'
Notice: Finished catalog run in 0.15 seconds
```

Log in to Foreman using the credentials you've got. After login, you will see a dashboard similar to the one shown in Figure 10-13.

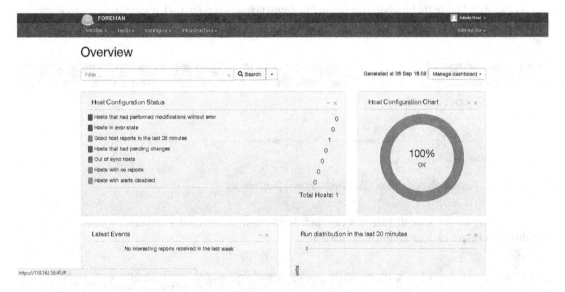

Figure 10-13. *Foreman dashboard*

As you can see in Figure 10-13, the dashboard shows the one host that you have just added. Before we move forward and install the ELK Stack using Foreman, you must install the ntp module for Foreman, as Puppet requires time accuracy. To install the module, change the directory to /opt/puppetlabs/ and run the following command:

```
[vishne0@puppet puppetlabs ~]$ sudo bin/puppet module install puppetlabs-ntp [sudo] password
for vishne0:
Notice: Preparing to install into /etc/puppet/environments/production/modules ...
Notice: Downloading from https://forgeapi.puppetlabs.com ...
Notice: Installing -- do not interrupt ...
/etc/puppet/environments/production/modules
puppetlabs-ntp (v4.2.0)
 puppetlabs-stdlib (v4.12.0)
```

The module is installed on your Puppet master server. Next, we will add it to Foreman. Open the Foreman admin console, and go to Configure ➤ Puppet Classes, as shown in Figure 10-14.

Figure 10-14. *Configure ➤ Puppet ➤ Classes*

As shown in Figure 10-14, when you are on the Puppet classes screen, click Import from [hostname] (Figure 10-15).

Figure 10-15. *Puppet classes screen. Click Import from [hostname]*

As you can see in Figure 10-15, when you click Import from [hostname], you will see a screen like the one shown in Figure 10-16, with the modules added.

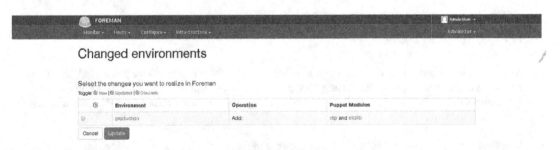

Figure 10-16. *Showing modules added in Foreman*

Figure 10-16 shows the modules that are now added in Foreman. You have to check the module and click Update (see Figure 10-17).

Figure 10-17. *Updating modules in Foreman*

As shown in Figure 10-17, once you click Update, you will see a screen similar to the one shown in Figure 10-18.

Puppet classes

Class name	Environments and documentation	Host groups	Hosts	Parameters	Variables	
ntp	production		0	50	0	Delete ▾
ntp::config			0	0	0	Delete
ntp::install			0	0	0	Delete
ntp::params			0	0	0	Delete
ntp::service			0	0	0	Delete
stdlib			0	0	0	Delete
stdlib::stages			0	0	0	Delete

Displaying all 7 entries

Figure 10-18. *ntp is installed*

The ntp module is now installed, as shown in Figure 10-18. If you want to edit the default settings of ntp, go to Puppet classes, click ntp, and then click the Smart Class Parameter tab, scroll down, and click servers. You will see a screen similar to the one shown in Figure 10-19.

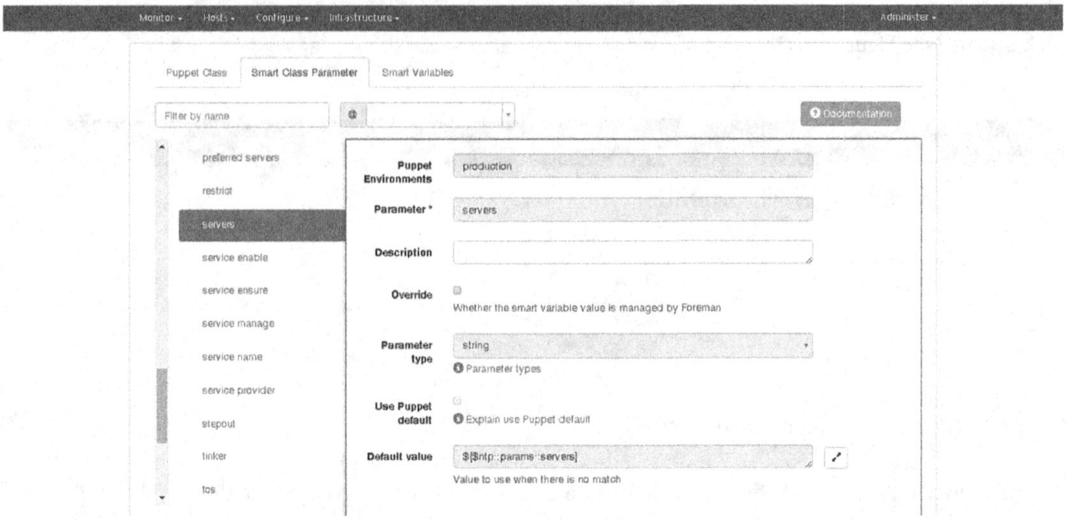

Figure 10-19. *Editing the default settings of ntp*

As shown in Figure 10-19, you can edit the ntp setting if you wish to do so. So now you are ready to install ntp on your managed hosts. Go to hosts ➤ All hosts ➤ Select the host and then click edit. There, click Puppet Classes, and you will see the available classes. In my case, I can see ntp and stdlib. Click ntp, and it will expand. Click the + (plus) sign in front of ntp, and it will add the module to Include Classes shown on the left side. Click the Submit button to save the changes. You have now added ntp (Figure 10-20).

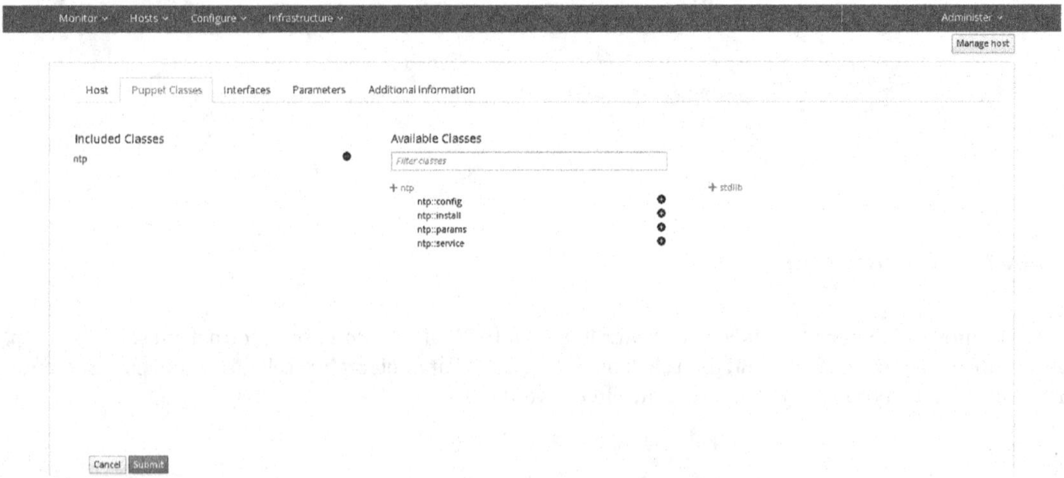

Figure 10-20. *Adding ntp*

As shown in Figure 10-20, you have added ntp, now change the directory to /opt/puppetlabs and run the Puppet agent again to see the changes, as follows:

```
[vishne0@puppet puppetlabs ~]$ sudo bin/puppet agent --test
[sudo] password for vishne0:
Info: Retrieving pluginfacts
Info: Retrieving plugin
Info: Loading facts
Info: Caching catalog for puppet.centylabs.com
Info: Applying configuration version '1473161198'
Notice: /Stage[main]/Ntp::Install/Package[ntp]/ensure: created
Notice: /Stage[main]/Ntp::Config/File[/etc/ntp.conf]/content:
--- /etc/ntp.conf       2016-05-31 10:11:10.000000000 +0000
+++ /tmp/puppet-file20160906-9595-u318fq        2016-09-06 11:26:44.388403291 +0000
@@ -1,58 +1,40 @@
-# For more information about this file, see the man pages
-# ntp.conf(5), ntp_acc(5), ntp_auth(5), ntp_clock(5), ntp_misc(5), ntp_mon(5).
+# ntp.conf: Managed by puppet.
+#
+# Enable next tinker options:
+# panic - keep ntpd from panicking in the event of a large clock skew
+# when a VM guest is suspended and resumed;
+# stepout - allow ntpd change offset faster
+tinker panic 0

-driftfile /var/lib/ntp/drift
+disable monitor

 # Permit time synchronization with our time source, but do not
 # permit the source to query or modify the service on this system.
-restrict default nomodify notrap nopeer noquery
+restrict default kod nomodify notrap nopeer noquery
+restrict -6 default kod nomodify notrap nopeer noquery
+restrict 127.0.0.1
+restrict -6 ::1
+
+
+
+# Set up servers for ntpd with next options:
+# server - IP address or DNS name of upstream NTP server
+# iburst - allow send sync packages faster if upstream unavailable
+# prefer - select preferrable server
+# minpoll - set minimal update frequency
+# maxpoll - set maximal update frequency
+server 0.centos.pool.ntp.org
+server 1.centos.pool.ntp.org
+server 2.centos.pool.ntp.org
+
+
+# Driftfile.
+driftfile /var/lib/ntp/drift
```

```
+
+
+
+
+
+
+

-# Permit all access over the loopback interface. This could
-# be tightened as well, but to do so would effect some of
-# the administrative functions.
-restrict 127.0.0.1
-restrict ::1
-
-# Hosts on local network are less restricted.
-#restrict 192.168.1.0 mask 255.255.255.0 nomodify notrap
-
-# Use public servers from the pool.ntp.org project.
-# Please consider joining the pool (http://www.pool.ntp.org/join.html).
-server 0.centos.pool.ntp.org iburst
-server 1.centos.pool.ntp.org iburst
-server 2.centos.pool.ntp.org iburst
-server 3.centos.pool.ntp.org iburst
-
-#broadcast 192.168.1.255 autokey       # broadcast server
-#broadcastclient                       # broadcast client
-#broadcast 224.0.1.1 autokey           # multicast server
-#multicastclient 224.0.1.1             # multicast client
-#manycastserver 239.255.254.254               # manycast server
-#manycastclient 239.255.254.254 autokey # manycast client
-
-# Enable public key cryptography.
-#crypto
-
-includefile /etc/ntp/crypto/pw
-
-# Key file containing the keys and key identifiers used when operating
-# with symmetric key cryptography.
-keys /etc/ntp/keys
-
-# Specify the key identifiers which are trusted.
-#trustedkey 4 8 42
-
-# Specify the key identifier to use with the ntpdc utility.
-#requestkey 8
-
-# Specify the key identifier to use with the ntpq utility.
-#controlkey 8
-
-# Enable writing of statistics records.
-#statistics clockstats cryptostats loopstats peerstats
```

```
-
-# Disable the monitoring facility to prevent amplification attacks using ntpdc
-# monlist command when default restrict does not include the noquery flag. See
-# CVE-2013-5211 for more details.
-# Note: Monitoring will not be disabled with the limited restriction flag.
-disable monitor

Info: Computing checksum on file /etc/ntp.conf
Info: /Stage[main]/Ntp::Config/File[/etc/ntp.conf]: Filebucketed /etc/ntp.conf to puppet
with sum dc9e5754ad2bb6f6c32b954c04431d0a
Notice: /Stage[main]/Ntp::Config/File[/etc/ntp.conf]/content: content changed '{md5}
dc9e5754ad2bb6f6c32b954c04431d0a' to '{md5}1f44e40bd99abd89f0a209e823285332'
Info: Class[Ntp::Config]: Scheduling refresh of Class[Ntp::Service]
Info: Class[Ntp::Service]: Scheduling refresh of Service[ntp]
Notice: /Stage[main]/Ntp::Service/Service[ntp]/ensure: ensure changed 'stopped' to 'running'
Info: /Stage[main]/Ntp::Service/Service[ntp]: Unscheduling refresh on Service[ntp]
Notice: Finished catalog run in 5.05 seconds
```

Now, when I ran Puppet again, it installed, configured itself, and restarted the service. Let's go back to your web GUI and see if it's showing any changes.

Go to Host ➤ All Hosts. You will then you see a reports screen (Figure 10-21). Click the top report, and you will see that it configured ntp.

Figure 10-21. *Foreman is installed and ntp is configured*

Simple, no? Now we will move on to the most important part: installing the ELK Stack using Foreman and Puppet.

Installing Logstash Using Puppet and Foreman

Issue the following command to install Logstash:

```
[vishne0@puppet ~]$ sudo puppet module install elasticsearch-logstash
Notice: Preparing to install into /etc/puppet/environments/production/modules ...
Notice: Downloading from https://forgeapi.puppetlabs.com ...
Notice: Installing -- do not interrupt ...
/etc/puppet/environments/production/modules
âââ¬ elasticsearch-logstash (v0.6.4)
  âââ electrical-file_concat (v1.0.1)
  âââ puppetlabs-stdlib (v4.12.0)
```

Now go to web GUI. Click Configure ➤ Puppet ➤ Classes and click Import from [hostname], as you did for ntp previously. Once you click Import [hostname], it will show you a Changed environments screen. Select the check box and click Submit. Once you click Submit, it will take you to the Puppet Classes page. You will see what changes you have to make in the default module settings in the next section.

Now, to add it to your host, go to Hosts ➤ All hosts and click edit, at the far right. Once you are on the screen, click Puppet Classes and you will see "logstash" in the list, as shown in Figure 10-22.

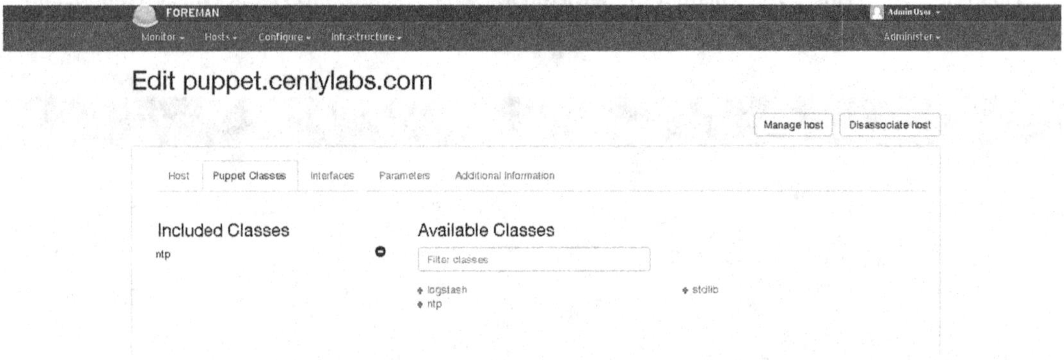

Figure 10-22. *Logstash module in Available Classes*

Click logstash, and it will expand. Then click the + (plus) sign to add it to Included Classes.

As shown in Figure 10-23, the Logstash module is added. To move ahead, you have to make some modifications in the Logstash module configuration.

Figure 10-23. *Logstash added*

Open the web GUI, and go to Configure ➤ Puppet Classes. Click logstash and then, on Smart Class Parameter, scroll down to manage repo. Check Override, then in Parameter type, select boolean and set the default value to true, as shown in Figure 10-24.

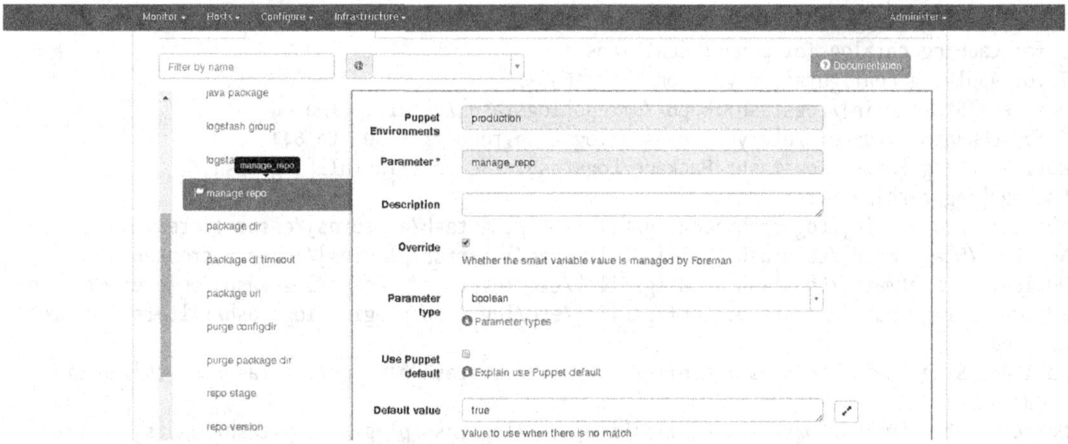

Figure 10-24. *Editing the Logstash* managerepo *parameter*

As seen in the figure, we have made two changes to the default settings. You also have to make sure that it installs Java, so click Java install and then check override and put true in the default value field, as shown in Figure 10-25.

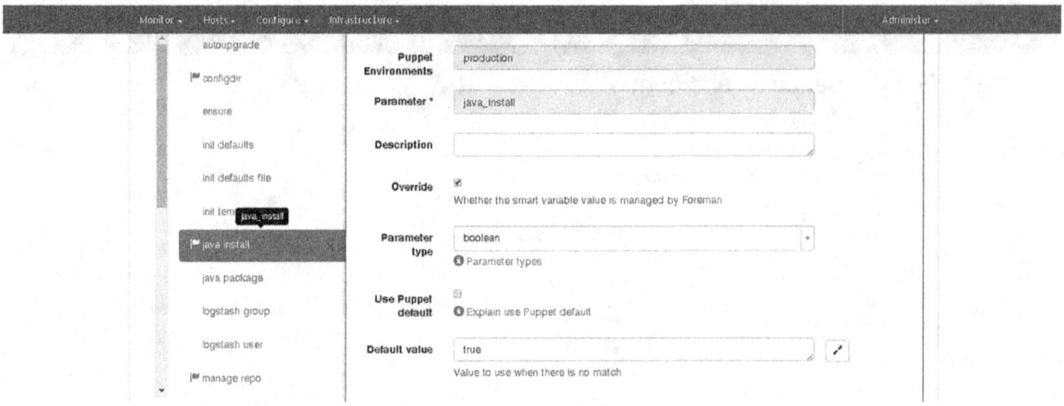

Figure 10-25. *Configuring Java install parameters for the Logstash module*

Once complete, click Submit and run the Puppet agent.

```
[vishne0@puppet puppetlabs]$ sudo bin/puppet agent --test
[sudo] password for vishne0:
Info: Retrieving pluginfacts
Info: Retrieving plugin
Info: Loading facts
Info: Caching catalog for puppet.centylabs.com
Info: Applying configuration version '1473165431'
Notice: /Stage[main]/Logstash::Repo/Yumrepo[logstash]/ensure: created
Info: changing mode of /etc/yum.repos.d/logstash.repo from 600 to 644
Notice: /Stage[main]/Logstash::Package/Logstash::Package::Install[logstash]/
Package[logstash]/ensure: created
Notice: /Stage[main]/Logstash::Config/File[/etc/logstash/patterns]/ensure: created
Notice: /Stage[main]/Logstash::Config/File[/etc/logstash/plugins]/ensure: created
Notice: /Stage[main]/Logstash::Config/File[/etc/logstash/plugins/logstash]/ensure: created
Notice: /Stage[main]/Logstash::Config/File[/etc/logstash/plugins/logstash/filters]/ensure:
created
Notice: /Stage[main]/Logstash::Config/File[/etc/logstash/plugins/logstash/codecs]/ensure:
created
Notice: /Stage[main]/Logstash::Config/File[/etc/logstash/plugins/logstash/inputs]/ensure:
created
Notice: /Stage[main]/Logstash::Config/File[/etc/logstash/plugins/logstash/outputs]/ensure:
created
Notice: /Stage[main]/Logstash::Config/File[/etc/logstash/conf.d/logstash.conf]/ensure:
defined content as '{md5}d41d8cd98f00b204e9800998ecf8427e'
Info: ls-config: Scheduling refresh of Class[Logstash::Service]
Info: Class[Logstash::Service]: Scheduling refresh of Logstash::Service::Init[logstash]
Info: Logstash::Service::Init[logstash]: Scheduling refresh of Service[logstash]
Notice: /Stage[main]/Logstash::Service/Logstash::Service::Init[logstash]/Service[logstash]/
ensure: ensure changed 'stopped' to 'running'
Info: /Stage[main]/Logstash::Service/Logstash::Service::Init[logstash]/Service[logstash]:
Unscheduling refresh on Service[logstash]
Notice: Finished catalog run in 23.82 seconds
```

```
Notice: /Stage[main]/Logstash::Java/Package[java-1.7.0-openjdk]/ensure: created
Notice: /Stage[main]/Logstash::Service/Logstash::Service::Init[logstash]/Service[logstash]/
ensure: ensure changed 'stopped' to 'running'
Info: /Stage[main]/Logstash::Service/Logstash::Service::Init[logstash]/Service[logstash]:
Unscheduling refresh on Service[logstash]
Notice: Finished catalog run in 20.70 seconds
[vishne0@puppet puppetlabs]$ java -version
openjdk version "1.8.0_102"
OpenJDK Runtime Environment (build 1.8.0_102-b14)
OpenJDK 64-Bit Server VM (build 25.102-b14, mixed mode)
```

Bingo!! Logstash and Java both are installed and configured. Let's check to see if we can start Logstash by default, as follows:

```
[vishne0@puppet puppet]$ sudo service logstash start

[vishne0@puppet puppet]$ ps aux | grep logstash
logstash 16662  100  4.6 1433088 94516 pts/0   SNl  12:50   0:05 java -XX:+UseParNewGC
-XX:+UseConcMarkSweepGC -Djava.awt.headless=true -XX:CMSInitiatingOccupancyFraction=75
-XX:+UseCMSInitia
tingOccupancyOnly -Djava.io.tmpdir=/var/lib/logstash -Xmx500m -Xss2048k -Djffi.boot.library.
path=/opt/logstash/vendor/jruby/lib/jni -XX:+UseParNewGC -XX:+UseConcMarkSweepGC -Djava.awt.
headles
s=true -XX:CMSInitiatingOccupancyFraction=75 -XX:+UseCMSInitiatingOccupancyOnly -Djava.
io.tmpdir=/var/lib/logstash -Xbootclasspath/a:/opt/logstash/vendor/jruby/lib/jruby.jar
-classpath : -Djr
uby.home=/opt/logstash/vendor/jruby -Djruby.lib=/opt/logstash/vendor/jruby/lib -Djruby.
script=jruby -Djruby.shell=/bin/sh org.jruby.Main --1.9 /opt/logstash/lib/bootstrap/
environment.rb logst
ash/runner.rb agent -f /etc/logstash/conf.d -l /var/log/logstash/logstash.log
vishne0  16694  0.0  0.1 112660  2380 pts/0   S+   12:50   0:00 grep --color=auto logstash
```

Yes! The Logstash is installation is complete, as you can see in Figure 10-26. You can now configure it as explained previously in Chapter 1.

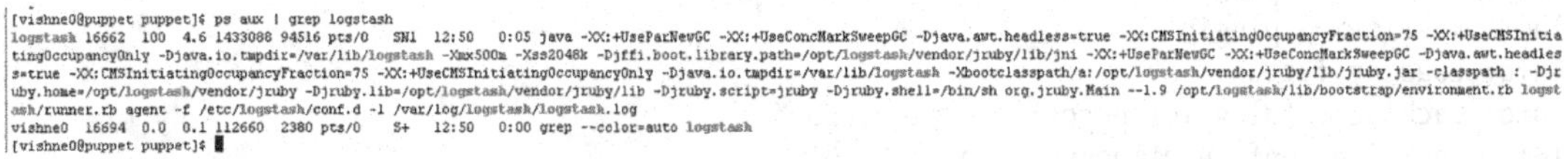

Figure 10-26. Running Logstash on Puppet master

Installing Elasticsearch Using Puppet and Foreman

We will now install Elasticsearch (Figure 10-27).

```
[vishne0@puppet puppetlabs]$ sudo bin/puppet module install elasticsearch-elasticsearch
[sudo] password for vishne0:
Notice: Preparing to install into /etc/puppet/environments/production/modules ...
Notice: Downloading from https://forgeapi.puppetlabs.com ...
Notice: Installing -- do not interrupt ...
/etc/puppet/environments/production/modules
elasticsearch-elasticsearch (v0.13.2)
 ceritsc-yum (v0.9.8)
 puppetlabs-apt (v2.3.0)
 puppetlabs-stdlib (v4.12.0)
 richardc-datacat (v0.6.2)
```

```
[vishne0@puppet puppetlabs]$ sudo bin/puppet module install elasticsearch-elasticsearch
Notice: Preparing to install into /etc/puppetlabs/code/environments/production/modules ...
Notice: Downloading from https://forgeapi.puppetlabs.com ...
Notice: Installing -- do not interrupt ...
/etc/puppetlabs/code/environments/production/modules
âââ┐ elasticsearch-elasticsearch (v0.13.2)
  âââ ceritsc-yum (v0.9.8)
  âââ puppetlabs-apt (v2.3.0)
  âââ puppetlabs-stdlib (v4.12.0)
  âââ richardc-datacat (v0.6.2)
```

Figure 10-27. *Installing the Elasticsearch plug-in using Puppet*

You have now installed the Elasticsearch plug-in, as shown in Figure 10-27. Run the Puppet agent, as follows:

```
[vishne0@puppet puppetlabs]$ sudo bin/puppet agent --test
[sudo] password for vishne0:
Info: Retrieving pluginfacts
Info: Retrieving plugin
Info: Loading facts
Info: Caching catalog for puppet.centylabs.com
Info: Applying configuration version '1473167384'
Notice: Finished catalog run in 0.60 seconds
```

Again, go to the web GUI and to Configure ➤ Puppet Classes, and click Import from [hostname]. Check on it, as shown in Figure 10-28, and click update.

Figure 10-28. *Elasticsearch module added to Foreman*

Go to Puppet Classes, click Elasticsearch, click manage repo, and then tick override. Also, change the default value to true and Key type to boolean. You must change the value of repo version. Scroll down and click on repo version, click override and put "2.x" in the Default value field. Now click Submit. Once again, go to Hosts ➤ All Hosts, and then go to edit and select Puppet Classes. Here, you will see that Elasticsearch is inside Available Classes. You must repeat the steps you completed for installing Logstash. Click Elasticsearch, then click the + (plus) sign in front of Elasticsearch, and it will add it to Included Classes (Figure 10-29).

Figure 10-29. *Elasticsearch added to Included Classes*

As shown in Figure 10-29, click Submit and run the Puppet agent again.

```
[vishne0@puppet puppetlabs]$ sudo bin/puppet agent --test
Info: Retrieving pluginfacts
Info: Retrieving plugin
Info: Loading facts
Info: Caching catalog for puppet.centylabs.com
Info: Applying configuration version '1473171508'
Notice: /Stage[main]/Elasticsearch::Repo/Yumrepo[elasticsearch]/baseurl: baseurl changed
'https://packages.elastic.co/elasticsearch/true/centos' to 'https://packages.elastic.co/
elasticsearch/2.x/centos'
Notice: /Stage[main]/Elasticsearch::Repo/Yumrepo[elasticsearch]/gpgkey: gpgkey changed
'https://packages.elastic.co/GPG-KEY-elasticsearch' to 'http://packages.elastic.co/GPG-KEY-
elasticsearch'
Info: /Stage[main]/Elasticsearch::Repo/Yumrepo[elasticsearch]: Scheduling refresh of
Exec[elasticsearch_yumrepo_yum_clean]
```

```
Info: /Stage[main]/Elasticsearch::Repo/Yumrepo[elasticsearch]: Scheduling refresh of
Exec[elasticsearch_yumrepo_yum_clean]
Notice: /Stage[main]/Elasticsearch::Repo/Exec[elasticsearch_yumrepo_yum_clean]: Triggered
'refresh' from 2 events
Notice: /Stage[main]/Elasticsearch::Package/Package[elasticsearch]/ensure: created
Info: /Stage[main]/Elasticsearch::Package/Package[elasticsearch]: Scheduling refresh of
Exec[remove_plugin_dir]
Notice: /Stage[main]/Elasticsearch::Package/Exec[remove_plugin_dir]: Triggered 'refresh'
from 1 events
Info: Computing checksum on file /etc/init.d/elasticsearch
Notice: /Stage[main]/Elasticsearch::Config/Augeas[/etc/sysconfig/elasticsearch]/returns:
executed successfully
```

Elasticsearch is installed as well. Before you go ahead and start Elasticsearch, there is one more thing that you must do. Just run the following command:

```
[vishne0@puppet puppetlabs]$ sudo /usr/bin/systemctl unmask elasticsearch
```

Installing Kibana Using Puppet and Foreman

Finally, let's install Kibana. Elasticsearch doesn't provide a Puppet module for Kibana, so we will search for the Kibana module at https://forge.puppet.com. The most downloaded module is lesaux/kibana4. Let's install that one now, as follows:

```
[vishne0@puppet puppetlabs]$ sudo bin/puppet module install lesaux-kibana4 Notice: Preparing
to install into /etc/puppet/environments/production/modules ...
Notice: Downloading from https://forgeapi.puppetlabs.com ...
Notice: Installing -- do not interrupt ...
/etc/puppet/environments/production/modules
lesaux-kibana4 (v1.0.17)
 puppetlabs-apt (v2.3.0)
```

Now go to web GUI, click Configure ➤ Puppet Classes and then click Import [hostname]. You will see the Kibana module that you have just installed. Now just check it and click Update. You have added the Kibana4 module, as shown in Figure 10-30.

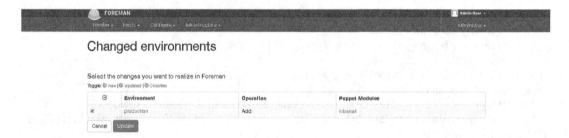

Figure 10-30. *Adding the Kibana module to Foreman*

Now that you are back to the Puppet Classes screen, click Kibana4. Click manage repo check override, then Submit. Go to Hosts ➤ All Hosts and click edit, at the far right of the host. Next, click the Puppet

Classes tab, then click Kibana4. It will expand. Now click the + (plus) sign in front of Kibana4. It will add it to Included Classes. Click Submit. It's time to run the Puppet agent again.

```
[vishne0@puppet /]$ sudo puppet agent --test
Info: Retrieving pluginfacts
Info: Retrieving plugin
Info: Loading facts
Info: Caching catalog for puppet.centylabs.com
Info: Applying configuration version '1473175172'
Notice: /Stage[main]/Kibana4::Install::Package/Yumrepo[kibana-4.5]/ensure: created
Info: changing mode of /etc/yum.repos.d/kibana-4.5.repo from 600 to 644
Notice: /Stage[main]/Kibana4::Install::Package/Package[kibana4]/ensure: created
Notice: /Stage[main]/Kibana4::Service/Service[kibana4]/ensure: ensure changed 'stopped' to 'running'
Info: /Stage[main]/Kibana4::Service/Service[kibana4]: Unscheduling refresh on
Service[kibana4]
Notice: Finished catalog run in 59.61 seconds
```

Good one! Kibana4 is now installed, configured, and it has started as well. You can access the GUI at http://yourip:5601.

As you can see in Figure 10-31, you can access the Kibana dashboard now.

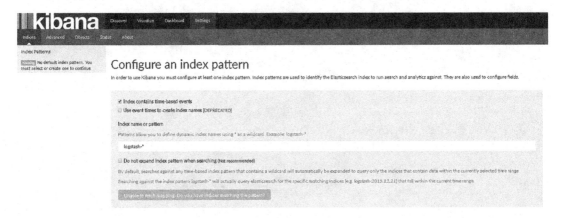

Figure 10-31. *Kibana configured using Puppet and Foreman*

Summary

In this chapter, you learned how to set up the ELK Stack using Puppet and Foreman. You configured the ELK Stack to have a centralized logging system in place for your remote servers and applications. You were also introduced to Puppet and Foreman, which give you more control and make it easier to maintain the ELK Stack and any other servers you wish to add.

You have learned how to install Puppet and Foreman in CentOS 7 and Ubuntu 16.04.1. You have also learned about

- Installing Foreman and Puppet
- Installing the ELK Stack modules for Puppet
- Configuring Foreman

Index

Get the eBook for only $4.99!

Why limit yourself?

Now you can take the weightless companion with you wherever you go and access your content on your PC, phone, tablet, or reader.

Since you've purchased this print book, we are happy to offer you the eBook for just $4.99.

Convenient and fully searchable, the PDF version enables you to easily find and copy code—or perform examples by quickly toggling between instructions and applications.

To learn more, go to http://www.apress.com/us/shop/companion or contact support@apress.com.

Printed in the United States
By Bookmasters